# THEY SAID YOU WERE TOO YOUNG

# *Upstage*

## THEY SAID YOU WERE TOO YOUNG

*Series Editor: Rony Robinson*

**Hodder & Stoughton**
LONDON SYDNEY AUCKLAND TORONTO

ISBN 0 340 50855 8

First published 1989

Selection and assignment material © 1989 Rony Robinson

*Tony and Donna* © Louise Page
*Lily and Colin* © Elisabeth Bond
*Mohicans* © Garry Lyons

Typeset by Litho Link Limited, Leighton, Welshpool, Powys, Wales.
Printed in Great Britain for the educational publishing division of
Hodder and Stoughton Ltd, Mill Road, Dunton Green, Sevenoaks,
Kent by Richard Clay Ltd, Bungay, Suffolk.

# Contents

# TOBY AND DONNA

*Louise Page*

Applications for performance of this play (amateur or professional) should be directed to Leah Schmidt, Curtis Brown Group, 162 Regent Street, London W1R 5TB.

## Cast

TOBY

DONNA

# Scene One

*Night. Just before eleven o'clock. A quiet street.* TOBY *and* DONNA, *waiting for the bus.*

DONNA: We were standing at the bus stop, and I was looking down the road and thinking that if you could go drinking, there were places you could go while late on a Saturday night, when Toby said –

TOBY: You've missed it.

DONNA: I haven't. It doesn't come while five to.

TOBY: Gone that.

DONNA: It hasn't.

But of course he has to check on his digital watch that lights up in the dark.

TOBY: Four minutes to. I tell you, it's gone early. They do, Saturday nights, so they don't have to pick up drunks coming out at closing time.

DONNA: Give it a bit longer.

So he walks about a bit, kicking at stones and stuff and I watched for the bus. I didn't want it to have gone.

*Pause.*

TOBY: I'm bored.

DONNA: You're always bored.

TOBY: Not my fault.

DONNA: He is always bored, Toby. He's always wanting to be doing something different. He's the sort that turns the telly over before the programme's finished, just because he's sick of watching that side.

TOBY: I'm going.

DONNA:    I didn't want him to go. It's lonely by yourself at that bus stop. Trees and stuff. Houses miles from the road.

I'm cold.

I thought that might make him cuddle me, but he kept his hands in his pockets.

TOBY:    Why don't you come back then, if you're cold?

DONNA:    I'm catching the bus.

TOBY:    I'm going.

DONNA:    Don't.

TOBY:    What's the point freezing, waiting for a bus that's gone?

DONNA:    You said, when we first went out, that you'd always see me home.

TOBY:    Yeah, well . . .

DONNA:    I made him promise because it isn't always nice for girls on the street at night, but boys don't seem to realize that.

Well what?

TOBY:    You might have said it were a lousy bus route where you lived.

DONNA:    'Tis from your house. Not from anywhere else. You promised.

TOBY:    Wouldn't have, if I'd known.

DONNA:    It's horrible, waiting at this stop by myself.

TOBY:    If you come up, me dad'll take you when they get back.

DONNA:    But I knew his dad had gone out drinking.

He'll have had a few. I'm not driving with him.

TOBY: My mum'll be okay. She's driving him. She'll drop you back.

DONNA: Will she?

TOBY: Yes.

DONNA: Sure?

TOBY: Yes. She will. You know she will. She always offers. She doesn't like you going home by yourself, you know that.

DONNA: I wouldn't have to go home by myself, if you took me.

TOBY: She'll take you.

DONNA: His mum, Debra, she does always offer. Sometimes I let her take me. She talks to me on the way home and it's a bit embarrassing. My mum doesn't ask me the sort of questions Debra does and she's the one that's supposed to. Toby's mum asks me things like: 'Do you know how to take care of yourself?' – things like that. And other things about sex. It's embarrassing when you don't hardly know somebody. She once told me why she'd been married four years before she had Toby's brother. She said, first there was the Berlin Wall and then there was Cuba and that's why her generation took to the Pill the way they did. I thought she was going to ask me about contraception and then she asked me if I thought I was going to die in my bed and I said that depended on if they dropped the atomic bomb while I were asleep.

*Pause.*

I felt a bit silly after saying that. She didn't say anything else 'til we got to my house. There's three boys in their family. She doesn't know about girls. She asks me to try and find out. Half the time, I never know what to tell her. Will you come with us when she takes me?

TOBY: Yes. I'm going. You coming or staying?

DONNA:  Don't have much choice, do I?

TOBY:  You wanted to see to the end of the film. If we'd watched the football, you could have caught the ten o'clock.

DONNA:  If you'd watched the football, I'd have got the eight o'clock.

*Pause.*

DONNA:  He walked right up to me to kiss me.

*Clock begins to strike eleven.*

You know I don't like it in the street.

TOBY:  Goodnight kiss.

*They kiss.*

DONNA:  He does kiss nice.

*The clock stops.*

I must have missed it.

TOBY:  Told you that ages ago.

DONNA:  Might as well come up to your house then, mightn't I?

TOBY:  Come on, then.

DONNA:  What time your mum and dad coming in?

*They start to go.*

TOBY:  Not late.

DONNA:  I'll have to telephone.

They don't wait up in our house, not like some parents. My dad leaves this alarm clock in the hall. It's set for half-past midnight. If we're not in by then to turn it off, it wakes him and there's hell to pay. My sister goes in, turns it off and goes out again. It's okay for her. There's loads of places she can go. Clubs and that.

# Scene Two

TOBY's *home. Kettle is whistling.* DONNA *is dialing her home.*

DONNA:  *(as she dials)*  I tell them if I'm going to be late. Saves arguing with them later.

*Phone is answered.*

It's Donna, dad. I'm at Toby's. The bus never came. We did. We waited ages. His mum'll bring me up when she gets home. She always offers. Yes. He says they'll be in by half-past. Yes. Okay. You know I always take enough money for a taxi. Okay. Bye.

*Phone down.*

TOBY:  Your coffee.

DONNA:  Ta. He says, if it gets to after twelve, I'm to take a taxi. They'll be in by then, won't they?

TOBY:  Probably. You didn't want sugar, did you?

DONNA:  No. I didn't know you could make coffee.

TOBY:  Why not?

DONNA:  Haven't ever seen you, that's all.

TOBY:  Never given me the chance.

DONNA:  You didn't offer when I was getting up and down in the middle of the film.

TOBY:  It was the ads.

DONNA:  Never time to boil a kettle during the ads. You always miss the first bit after.

TOBY:  You kept saying, 'Shall I make a coffee?'.

DONNA:  Didn't notice you offering.

TOBY:   Didn't want one.

DONNA:   You drank them.

TOBY:   Only because you'd made them.

DONNA:   I didn't want them, neither. Me dad says to my mum, 'Put the kettle on, lass'. They have a cup of tea nearly every break. Mum keeps saying she's going to bring the tea things in the lounge. Me dad says the pile'll come out of the carpet if it gets boiling water on it. He doesn't ever make his own.

TOBY:   I'm really domestic. I can make omelettes and stuff, you know.

DONNA:   You've never made me one.

TOBY:   Didn't know you wanted one. Make you one now, if you like.

DONNA:   This is fine, thanks.

*She drinks her coffee.*

TOBY:   It's proper coffee, you know.

DONNA:   It was nice coffee. Hot milk and everything. I knew he was trying to be nice to me.

It's okay.

*They sip.*

TOBY:   I'd like to be a chef.

DONNA:   You what?

TOBY:   You know, cooking things.

DONNA:   What do you want to do cooking for?

TOBY:   It's a good job.

DONNA:   No-one told you there aren't going to be any jobs?

TOBY:   People always have to eat. They need people to cook for them.

DONNA: They want fancy cooking. How are you going to learn that?

TOBY: I'm going to college for it.

DONNA: Where?

TOBY: Haven't decided. Away from here. I'd like to go to London. Somewhere like that.

DONNA: What'd happen to us?

TOBY: I could come home weekends.

DONNA: Oh.

*Pause.*

You really want to go away?

TOBY: Not much point going to college if you stop at home, is there?

DONNA: No.

TOBY: Be awful.

DONNA: I thought he was going to be a butcher like his dad and brother. Didn't know he wanted to go away. We'd never talked about it. I thought I'd miss him if he went. Girls whose lads have gone to college have an awful time. They know the lads are playing the field. They can't because they've stopped at home, everybody'd know.

You'll have to stop here while you do your A-levels.

*Pause.*

TOBY: Will you miss me?

*He fumbles with her.*

DONNA: Don't!

TOBY: Won't you?

DONNA:   I'm trying to drink my coffee.

He was trying to get his hand between my cardi. and my blouse.

TOBY:   I like you, Donna. I really do.

DONNA:   So you say. Hey!

TOBY:   Shall I put a record on?

DONNA:   If you like.

TOBY:   Anything particular you want?

DONNA:   Don't mind.

TOBY *puts on record.*

TOBY:   You'll like this.

DONNA:   I knew it was going to be something romantic.
They've got dimmer switches and everything at his house, and Tiffany lampshades – they haven't got round to paper ones at our house. He turned the dimmer switch 'til it was pitch black.

What you doing? I feel like I'm in a coal mine.

TOBY *gropes his way to settee.*

Mind!

TOBY:   Sorry.

DONNA:   What they going to say when they get back and find us in the dark?

TOBY:   What?

DONNA:   You can see from the street whether this light's on or not.

TOBY:   Nice in the dark.

DONNA:   I hate the dark. Can't we just have it dim?

TOBY:   Okay.

*He gets up and bangs into something.*

DONNA:   What you done?

TOBY:   Nothing. Banged the table, that's all.

DONNA:   So then, he turns the light up like it's floodlighting at Hillsborough.

Don't be daft. Like that. It's nice, like that. I bet from the street it looks like we're watching TV.

TOBY:   *(back to sofa)*   You comfortable?

DONNA:   Yes.

TOBY:   You sure?

DONNA:   Yes.

TOBY:   You can stretch yourself out a bit if you want.

DONNA:   I'm very comfortable, thank you.

TOBY:   Good.

DONNA:   Yes.

TOBY:   I really fancy you.

DONNA:   I fancy you and all.

TOBY:   Really?

DONNA:   Yes.

And I do because he isn't bad to look at. He doesn't have sort of spots or anything. He's got a blackhead on his nose but you can only see that when you're close up. And most of the time you're kissing him, you don't really notice. A lot of girls at school fancy him because he's quite nice. He's a good dancer as well. At school, we sort of had this disco at Christmas. It was more friendly than a disco because everybody knew everybody and you could only take one guest who wasn't in school. I'd seen him around but he was in the year above and it's difficult getting talking to them. I think that's why they had the disco. Me and my friends, we were wearing these party hats. Not sort of paper ones like you get in crackers. They were plastic but in miniature. Mine was like a postman's. Toby was making all these jokes about postman's knock. We were being really silly so we played it. He was a really nice kisser. After that, we were seeing each other.

TOBY *lights gas.*

What you putting the fire on for?

TOBY:    Thought you might be cold.

DONNA:    I'm fine.

TOBY:    I'm a bit cold.

DONNA:    I'll have to take my cardigan off. You'll have to mind.

It was an excuse to make him move. I'd got cramp in my arm from him lying on it.

*Takes off cardigan.*

TOBY:    That nice?

DONNA:    Yes.

TOBY:    Good.

DONNA:    It was nice lying there, listening to the record. In films, they always smoke when they're listening to music but we don't.

DONNA:    Hey, what do you think you're trying to do?

TOBY:    What's it feel like?

DONNA:    It felt like he'd got his hand half-way up my leg.

TOBY:   Like that?

DONNA:   It's alright.

TOBY:   That all?

DONNA:   Your hands are cold.

TOBY:   Cold hands, warm heart.

DONNA:   Could just be because you don't wear gloves when you go out.

*Pause.*

TOBY:   Nice music, isn't it?

DONNA:   Yes.

*Pause.*

Do you always put this on when you're with girls?

TOBY:   Do you mean my shirt or the music?

DONNA:   It's a nice shirt. Sort of soft. Brushed cotton.

TOBY:   My gran got it me for Christmas.

DONNA:   I've never seen you wear it before.

TOBY:   Been saving it.

DONNA:   What for?

TOBY:   Special occasion.

DONNA:   Such as?

TOBY:   Tonight.

DONNA:   We haven't even been out.

TOBY:   You were coming round.

DONNA:   You dressed up just for me coming round?

TOBY:   Yes. Thought you'd like it. I had a bath as well.

DONNA:  Did you?

TOBY:  You smell really nice. Why don't you take your shoes off?

DONNA:  Why?

TOBY:  You could put your feet up if you took your shoes off.

DONNA:  Okay.

*Sound of* DONNA *taking off shoes and dropping them.*

TOBY:  Nice and wide this settee, isn't it? Like a bed almost.

DONNA:  Yes.

TOBY:  Pulls out into a bed you know.

DONNA:  Does it?

TOBY:  When people stop.

DONNA:  We've got a put-u-up. It's not as comfortable as this.

TOBY:  Do you want me to show you how it makes into a bed?

DONNA:  It was so obvious what he was getting at.

 Your mum and dad'll be back.

TOBY:  They're stopping over at me Auntie Jean's.

DONNA:  What? You told me they were coming back.

TOBY:  They are – tomorrow.

DONNA:  You said your mother would take me home.

TOBY:  She will, when she comes back.

DONNA:  You said she was coming back tonight.

TOBY:  I never did.

DONNA:  You lied.

TOBY:   Never said they were coming back tonight. You just assumed that.

DONNA:   You didn't tell me different.

TOBY:   Didn't ask me.

DONNA:   How am I supposed to get home?

TOBY:   You can stay.

DONNA:   Maybe I don't want to.

TOBY:   You can get a taxi.

DONNA:   Where am I going to get the money for a taxi?

TOBY:   Told your dad you had the money for one.

DONNA:   Only so he didn't worry. Where'd I get money for taxis?

TOBY:   Lend you it then.

DONNA:   Lend it me?

TOBY:   All right. I'll go halves with you.

DONNA:   Why should I have to pay anything?

TOBY:   You wanted to come back.

DONNA:   You said your mum would run me home, Toby Jordon.

TOBY:   I'll give you the money for a taxi then.

DONNA·   You got a number?

TOBY:   Don't ring for one yet.

DONNA:   Get off.

TOBY:   Donna.

DONNA:   Leave off.

TOBY:   What have I done now?

DONNA:   I were so mad I could have killed him.

TOBY:   Give us a kiss, Donna.

*He tries to kiss her.*

DONNA:   You've a blackhead on your nose. You know that?

TOBY:   Donna . . .

DONNA:   It's horrible to look at.

TOBY:   You mad at me?

DONNA:   What do you think?

TOBY:   I thought you'd like it with no-one here.

DONNA:   There's been no-one here all night.

TOBY:   You kept saying you wanted to watch the film.

DONNA:   I was. I like seeing the end of them.

*Pause.*

TOBY:   You could have a drink if you wanted.

DONNA:   Don't they mind?

TOBY:   No. So long as I don't go mad, they never notice what's gone. You can have anything you like.

DONNA:   You having one?

TOBY:   Might as well.

DONNA:   Yes. What you got then?

TOBY:   Most things.

DONNA:   I don't want one that makes your breath smell. What you having?

TOBY:   Vodka and lime.

DONNA:  I don't mind that. I want a lot of lime.

TOBY:  Okay. The lime's in the fridge. I won't be a minute.

*Exit* TOBY.

DONNA:  *(shouting after him)*  I'm only staying while twelve. I
mean it.
He was really ages getting the lime. When he came back,
he had these two great nail marks on his nose where he'd
squeezed his blackhead.

TOBY:  Vodka and lime. You can lie back down now.

DONNA:  I can't drink lying down.

TOBY:  Donna . . .

DONNA:  I'm going at twelve.

TOBY:  Go later.

DONNA:  I've got to work tomorrow morning.

Sunday mornings I help out at this hotel. Making beds and
such. Better than a Saturday job. Means you can go to town
on Saturdays. I like it. But sometimes you get odd men.
You have to watch them. Some of the other girls have seen
it all. You wouldn't believe it.

TOBY:  I think you're really attractive.

*She giggles.*

I'm not just telling you that. Do you love me?

DONNA:  I don't know.

TOBY:  I love you.

DONNA:  He'd only had two sips of his drink.

TOBY:  Donna . . .

DONNA:  He put his hand up my skirt.

TOBY:    Do you love me?

DONNA:    Don't know.

TOBY:    What you going out with me for, if you don't?

DONNA:    I like going out with you.

> I do as well. It's nice to have someone to go out with. Everyone else has.

TOBY:    I really do fancy you.

DONNA:    You keep saying.

TOBY:    D'you believe me?

DONNA:    You're squashing me.

TOBY:    Don't you believe me?

DONNA:    I believe you. Will you move?

> *He moves.*

> So he moved. I got one breath and he was squashing me again.

TOBY:    Will you, then?

DONNA:    I can't breathe.

TOBY:    Will you 'all the way'?

DONNA:    What?

TOBY:    You know.

DONNA:    I knew what he meant but . . .

TOBY:    If you love me.

DONNA:    I didn't say that.

TOBY:    Don't you?

DONNA:    I'm not sixteen.

TOBY:   Doesn't stop other girls.

DONNA:   Have you been with other girls?

TOBY:   Well . . .

DONNA:   Well?

TOBY:   No.

DONNA:   Never know if you're telling the truth or not.

TOBY:   I haven't.

DONNA:   Truly?

TOBY:   Promise. I'll be really careful.

DONNA:   I don't know.

TOBY:   You can't get pregnant first time, you know.

DONNA:   That's not what they taught at school, is it?

TOBY:   You can't.

DONNA:   Who says?

TOBY:   Nobody gets caught first time.

DONNA:   I know girls who have.

TOBY:   They've been lying, then.

DONNA:   Who says?

TOBY:   Just the first time they got caught. Probably been doing it for ages. Donna . . .

DONNA:   He was really squashing me and breathing right in my face.

TOBY:   Donna . . .

DONNA:   I don't know . . .

TOBY:   Don't you fancy me?

DONNA:   Yes . . .

TOBY:   Come on, then.

DONNA:   I don't want to.

TOBY:   Won't take long.

DONNA:   Not that.

TOBY:   You have to begin sometime.

DONNA:   No.

TOBY:   You'll be okay. I'll make sure.

DONNA:   *(frightened)*   I don't want to.

TOBY:   Most girls would.

DONNA:   Thank you.

TOBY:   Donna . . .

DONNA:   I'm not sixteen.

TOBY:   Couple of months you will be.

DONNA:   That's two months. Can't you just wait two months?

TOBY:   Why?

*Pause.*

You saying you will in two months?

DONNA:   But I didn't know if I'd even be seeing him then.

Perhaps.

TOBY:   You just said you would.

DONNA:   I never did.

TOBY:   I get other girls throwing themselves at me.

*Pause.*

Susan really fancies me.

DONNA:    Susan had said that. She was really jealous when she knew Toby was seeing me.

DONNA:    She's a slag.

TOBY:    I think she's very sexy.

DONNA:    I don't want to.

So he got up off the settee.

TOBY:    *(getting off settee)*    You might as well go home, then.

DONNA:    I will.

*Pause.*

Can I have the money for the taxi?

*Pause.*

You said you were giving me the money for the taxi.

TOBY:    After the way you've just treated me?

DONNA:    You said if I stayed, you would.

TOBY:    You haven't stayed.

DONNA:    There's staying and staying, isn't there?

TOBY:    There is and you haven't.

DONNA:    Why should I have to, for my taxi fare?

TOBY:    Shouldn't have come then, should you?

DONNA:    You said your mum would take me up.

TOBY:    Well, I was wrong.

DONNA:    You mean, you lied.

*Pause.*

Will you walk me home, then?

TOBY: It's too cold. And we're not seeing each other any more, are we?

DONNA: Aren't we?

TOBY: No point, is there?

DONNA: Isn't there?

TOBY: Not that I can see.

DONNA: Five minutes ago you were saying you loved me.

TOBY: Well . . .

DONNA: He just looked at me. He is attractive. Lots of girls say so. Really pretty ones. Better looking girls than me. They think he's attractive. I'm lucky really, going out with him. And he is a lovely kisser.

*Up music.*

# LILY AND COLIN

*Elisabeth Bond*

Applications for performance of this play (amateur or professional) should be directed to Joy Westendarp, ICB Ltd, Suite 8, 26 Charing Cross Road, London WC2H 0DG.

## *Cast*

LILY

COLIN

TRAIN ANNOUNCER

TUCKER

TRAIN GUARD

LILY'S FATHER

SHOPWOMAN

ADA

EDIE

VICAR

VICAR'S WIFE

POLICEMEN

POLICEWOMAN

STATION GUARD

*There are station noises in the background –*
*announcements, etc. Taxis drawing up, doors slamming.*
COLIN *is whistling, with a feeble effort to be jaunty. There*
*are running footsteps.*

LILY:   *(breathless)*   Colin! I've come! I've come, my love, I've
come!

COLIN:   I'd nearly given you up.

LILY:   Oh no. Never.

COLIN:   You were a very long time. Twelve o'clock, you said.
I've been waiting here twenty-five minutes, and already
one or two people have been observing me.

LILY:   I'm sorry, my love, don't fret.

COLIN:   Once you've been observed, there only needs to be a
bit of unpleasantness and before you know it, you're at the
police station, trying to answer their questions.

LILY:   And you'd say, I'm waiting for my lover.

COLIN:   They'd say you were too young.

LILY:   It's not age that counts.

COLIN:   Experience of life counts, I know that. But they'd still
say thirteen was too young.

*Pause.*

LILY:   I met Albert Stringer. He said he'd give me a good price
for them teaspoons if I met him at t'Ring of Bells for twelve
o'clock. That's what kept me. But it were worth it. They're
right cheating buggers, all of them, but Albert used to deal
wi' me nana and he's better than most. Look what he give
me.

COLIN:   Not now, Lily, not here.

LILY: No-one's looking. Me nana always kept her money down her bra. Want to look!

COLIN: No . . . No . . . Will you put it away . . . Oh God.

LILY: It's alright! I'm quite decent.

COLIN: I'm sorry, but I see doom and disaster lurking round every corner.

LILY: It's only yer nerves, imagining things.

COLIN: I know I'm weak . . .

LILY: You're not weak, you're sensitive.

COLIN: I might have done something I shouldn't if you hadn't come when you did.

*There is a train announcement, clearly heard:* 'The next train to call at Platform 4 is the 12.58 to London Euston, calling at Wigan, Warrington, Crewe and London Euston . . .' *The announcement continues in the background:* ' . . . with connections at Crewe for Birmingham, North Wales, Bristol and the West of England. This train is running approximately eight minutes late.'

LILY: London, eh! We could go to London if we wanted. I nicked a tenner off me dad. We could still go and have some to spare.

COLIN: There you are again! I thought we were going to the English Lake District. That's what we discussed – I've even brought the leaflet.

LILY: Of course we are.

COLIN: London holds a lot of temptations to the unwary – pottery, silverware, ladies silk headscarves . . . I've already been there, you've seen my tea-towel. And it's not only London, it's Westminster Abbey, the National Gallery, River Thames. Once you get down there, the list is endless. It's best kept away from.

LILY:   It's alright, Colin, it's alright. Only a joke.

COLIN:   If we got to the English Lake District, at least I can add
to my collection – a mug, say, or even another egg-cup.
Look, it says so on the leaflet . . . 'also attractive souvenirs'
. . . something to commemorate my visit.

LILY:   Our visit, Colin. We're both going, together.

COLIN:   I'm worried, that's all, worried. You're so young, and
I . . .

LILY:   We're strong in each other.

COLIN:   I have these tendencies, you know I have.

LILY:   Remember!

*Pause.*

Go and get t'tickets, Colin. One and a half to the English
Lakes. Single, because we're never coming back – we're
going on.

*Pause.*

COLIN:   The Scottish Highlands?

LILY:   The Yorkshire Dales.

COLIN:   They've some good class souvenirs in the Yorkshire
Dales.

LILY:   The, er . . . the mountains of Wales.

COLIN:   Glorious Devon.

LILY:   And when our money's run out, we'll thumb it. Brrm
brrm, brrm brrm. Give us a lift, mate, wherever you're
going; we don't mind.

COLIN:   Train's best. I prefer to travel by train.

LILY:   We'll travel like lords, by train, by coach – travelling like
lords.

COLIN:    So you wait here, Lily, while I get the tickets.

*There is a brief fade. Then, a shout: 'Barrow train. Any more for Barrow? Barrow train!'. Train doors slam, the whistle blows. The train moves off.*

*Train noises as before but from inside the train. There are footsteps along the corridor and the carriage door sliding back.*

LILY:    This'll do. I'll put my carrier down on this side, then people will think we're full.

COLIN:    I don't think there are many.

LILY:    I'm going to look round.

*The door slides back, footsteps, train noises, footsteps again.*

There's an old couple at the end, and we're right next to t'toilet. I'll go in there.

*Door and footsteps again.*

Two bog rolls, a bit of soap and some of them paper towels. Do you want them in your carrier, or shall I put them in mine?

COLIN:    You keep them.

LILY:    I took our Nancy's cassette recorder. Stupid cow, she's always been nasty to me. She'll be mad when she finds it gone. And I took a tin of peaches, a tin of milk, a packet of fags and some matches, so we'll be alright.

*Train noises.*

COLIN:    Did you leave a note to say you'd left?

LILY:    I'll send me dad a picture postcard when we get to the English Lakes. 'Colin and me are having a lovely time. Glad you're not here.'

*Pause. Train noises.*

Oh, Colin, it's so long since I've been on a train. T'last time were with me nana. She took me to Blackpool once.

COLIN:  Blackpool Tower, the Golden Mile?

LILY:  I don't remember them. I just remember t'train. Packed it was, packed out. And it wasn't a proper train; not like this, where you have your own little compartment to yourselves, like your own home, like a caravan. I wouldn't mind living in a caravan, except that for us the view out of t'window would always be different. Look now, we're going past them bungalows. A girl at our school lives in a bungalow like them. She thinks she's it.

*Pause. Train noises.*

Eh, Colin. You could sleep on that side, I could sleep on this. Let's try it, shall we? Let's lie down.

*The seat creaks.*

Feels nice, doesn't it, rocking along? Try something on the cassette.

COLIN:  You do it. I'm not accustomed to these things.

LILY:  Give it here, then. I wonder what she's got in it.

*Click as she presses the cassette button. Loud pop music comes out, which LILY turns down a bit.*

This time yesterday I were thinking, this time tomorrow I'll be on t'train wi' my lover, speeding through the countryside.

COLIN:  The unspoilt English countryside.

LILY:  And this time three days ago, I were thinking, in three days time I'll be on t'train, and I never said a word to nobody.

COLIN:  It's always best to keep things to yourself.

LILY:   And now here I am. I can see t'sky upside down.

*Pause. Music, with train noises in the background.*

COLIN:   I used to see angels in the sky when I was little. Very foolishly I told my aunty's son – well, she wasn't really my aunty, but I had to call her aunty – I told her Melvin about the angels. That's how it got around. But I did see them. The sky was lit up and the surrounding countryside illuminated by them, but no-one saw them except me.

Of course, they laughed at me. I told my aunty's son – well, she wasn't really my aunty, but I had to call her aunty – I told her Melvin about the angels and that's how it got around. But I did see them, and no-one else did.

LILY:   I used to think the angel was my mum. Daft, eh! I were only young.

*Long pause. The cassette comes to an end. Train noises.*

Pity we can't be together int it, cuddled up close?

COLIN:   No . . . er, no . . . I think it's a very nice arrangement as it is.

LILY:   There's even blinds.

*Sound of blinds being pulled down.*

Now we're really private.

*She giggles and plumps down next to* COLIN.

Put your arm round me. Go on. You're so shy, Colin.

COLIN   Let's say, I'm rather reserved.

LILY:   You don't have to be shy wi' me. You could do anything you like wi' me and I wouldn't mind. Go on, do something.

COLIN:   I wouldn't like to feel I was taking advantage.

LILY:   Go on! What do you want to do? I'm all yours. I'll take me knickers off, if you like.

COLIN:   No, no. Don't do that.

LILY:   Why not?

COLIN:   My passion could easily run away with me and I wouldn't be answerable to the consequences. I prefer to keep a hold on myself, while I can.

LILY:   Nothing you could do would shock me. I'm unshockable.

*Pause.*

My uncle used to mess me around. I were only eight. I didn't know what he were doing. I though all uncles did that. I told me nan and she sorted him out.

*Pause.*

I miss nana. I hate me dad and I hate me sister. It were only her that I loved.

COLIN:   Don't, Lily, don't . . .

LILY:   And now, I've got you, and I love you.

COLIN:   Little Lily, eh? Little, little Lily.

*Police station. Office hum (phones, etc.) in background. Two-way radio crackling.*

TUCKER:   As soon as my wife died I got rid of them all. I didn't want sitting tenants devaluing the property, 'specially not that bunch. I've got plans for that house, high-class plans. Colin was the last one. I told him I wanted him out by tomorrow. I wasn't having him hanging round my neck. Of course, he didn't like it. I could tell he didn't. It would have suited him down to the ground to stay and keep his little racket going. Ten pounds a week he pocketed off the Social, ten bloody pounds! That might be worth you

looking into and all. I'm not blaming my wife, of course
I'm not. She was a big hearted woman, God bless her. It's
him! Thieving little rat. Christ knows what he's done me
out of over these last two years. Pretends he's religous,
that's his line. Many times I've caught him with his fingers
into something and he'd start bloody praying; 'God's on
my side', he'd say.

Of course, you know why he took my teaspoons, don't
you? Revenge! He doesn't like me. He even tried to set my
wife against me – tried his religion on her. Well, it doesn't
work with me. I'm not some woman he can twist himself
round. Colin bloody Beaumont! There's another thing
you could well afford to look into, and that's the girl.
What're you going to do about her? Kid of thirteen. Make
no mistake about it, he'll have gone off with her
somewhere. There must be a law against that. She's under
age, isn't she? What is it now – sixteen, seventeen? She's
hardly fourteen. He's a creep, Colin is; sticky-fingered,
one of them. You find the girl and you'll find Colin, and I
hope you'll find my bloody teaspoons.

POLICEMAN:   What was this girl's name?

TUCKER:   Wait a minute . . . what was her name? A thin little
thing, dark-haired, miserable looking . . . Lily! That was
it, Lily!

POLICEMAN:   You don't know where she came from?

TUCKER:   I'd be round there if I did.

POLICEMAN:   How did she come to meet Colin?

TUCKER:   God knows. On the street, I should imagine – she
had the look of the street about her, a gutter-snipe, if you
know what I mean. Then she turned up at our house, said
her dad had beaten her up. You don't need to think you
can stay here, I told her but, of course, Colin got round
the wife and she let her stop. Only for one night, mind.
They wouldn't have got away with more.

POLICEMAN: What makes you think she's gone off with this Colin Beaumont?

TUCKER: He was talking to her in the kitchen, saying he wanted to travel to the Lake District, to London. I never listened to his rubbish.

POLICEMAN: Where did she sleep that night?

TUCKER: Ah now . . . I was very careful about that . . . on the sofa in the back room. It was my wife, she was like that, do anyone a good turn. You couldn't reason with her.

POLICEMAN: Just a minute, Mr Tucker. *(Speaking into intercom)* I've got a gentleman here, a Mr Tucker, come in to report a theft. It seems the person involved might also be connected with the abduction of a young girl . . . If you would . . . Okay . . . *(To* TUCKER*)* Someone from the CID will be along to ask you a few questions. Won't keep you long.

TUCKER: Glad to help. Glad to do what I can. Types like that should be locked up. They're a menace, a bloody menace.

*Back to the train. The sound of blinds being pulled up.*

LILY: The sea! Look, Colin, there's the sea! Everywhere you look it's sea and sand.

*The carriage door slides back.*

Open the window, Colin and sniff up the sea.

*There is the sound of the corridor window being dragged open. There is a loud rushing noise from the air, which the voices have to battle against.*

COLIN: *(shouts)* This is the Christian path that we're following, across the sands.

LILY: What's that?

COLIN: Back in historical time. History!

LILY:   Good Queen Bess?

COLIN:   Across the sands!

*Train noises loud, then window is shut and voices back to normal again.*

COLIN:   They fled from ignorance and persecution, beckoned onwards by Jesus Christ.

LILY:   Like us, Colin!

COLIN:   See those hills on your right? That's the English Lake District. They found shelter and repose amongst those hills; they found rest for their souls.

*Pause.*

Often their enemies used to pursue them but they were swallowed up in the quicksands, whereas God showed the Christians the right path, beckoning them on in the person of Jesus Christ, Our Lord.

LILY:   *(sigh of happiness)*   Oh, Colin, you know so much.

*Pause.*

COLIN:   I remember expressing an interest to a chaplain I knew once. I said to him at the time, I often feel persecuted myself.

LILY:   And what did he say?

COLIN:   He said I might feel very suited in Barrow-in-Furness and he'd enquire about lodgings there. Of course, he never did.

*Pause.*

LILY:   I'm hungry, let's have a fag.

*Rustle of paper, match striking, etc.*

COLIN:   I've always taken an interest in history.

LILY:  Your souvenirs are historical, if you think about it.

COLIN:  Exactly.

*Pause. Train noises.*

LILY:  Me dad won't notice I've gone 'til he wants me to get him fags, then he'll start hollering – 'Lily, go and get us twenty Park Drive. Where's that bloody little cow?' – And he'll keep on 'til he goes out to t'pub. Then, when he gets back, he'll be too drunk to notice and I'll be far away.

COLIN:  What would your dad say if he knew you were with me?

LILY:  You're much too gentle and nice for him. He'd start mouthing off straight away.

COLIN:  You get people like him. There was a lorry driver at some lodgings I had. He used to say he wanted to smash my face in. It was most unpleasant sharing a room with him.

LILY:  Was he a drinker?

COLIN:  They usually are. And he was a dirty type. I believe in keeping myself clean – even under the most adverse circumstances I've always done my best, but he used to flaunt himself in his filth.

LILY:  How do you mean?

COLIN:  He used to hold me down and wave his socks under my nose. It was his idea of a joke when he'd had a few drinks. I had to move out in the end. They were nice lodgings too, some of the better ones.

LILY:  He sounds like my dad, just a big bully. You want to keep well away from types like that.

COLIN:  Oh, I try to.

*Pause.*

LILY:   When I send that postcard to him, I'm going to put 'hate, Lily' on the end. 'Having a lovely time. Glad you're not here. Hate, Lily.'

*Pause. Train noises, whistle blows. More train noises.*

Colin, am I the first person you told about them angels since the boy that laughed?

COLIN:   Oh yes.

LILY:   Ah.

*Footsteps along corridor. Door slides back.*

GUARD:   Tickets, please. You know this is a non-smoker, don't you?

LILY:   There's no-one here to bother.

GUARD:   If you want to smoke, you go next door. Otherwise, you put those cigarettes out.

LILY:   What if we don't?

COLIN:   No, Lily, no. We don't want to incur the wrath of officialdom. Alright, officer, anything you say.

GUARD:   And you're on the wrong train. Your tickets say Windermere, this is the Barrow train.

LILY:   We asked for the English Lake District.

GUARD:   Singles, are they? That'll be . . . £3.50 and £2 – £5.50 altogether; that's if you get off at the next station.

LILY:   We've already paid.

GUARD:   And you'll have to pay again.

LILY:   If you think we can't afford it, you're wrong.

GUARD:   I don't think anything. You might get a refund if you hand these tickets in, but you'll have to pay up now.

LILY: I don't see why we should.

COLIN: Gateway to the heartland of the English Lakes. It's written on this leaflet if you'd care to look. You see, *Gateway to the Heartland of the English Lakes*, published by the English Countryside Commission. I showed it to the gentleman in the ticket office and asked for one and a half to the English Lakes, and that's what he gave me.

GUARD: I don't care about your leaflet. All I know is that you are on the Barrow train and your tickets say Windermere.

COLIN: Excuse me, I also made enquiries on the platform.

LILY: You showed them the leaflet, didn't you, Colin?

COLIN: And the man indicated this train, Platform 5, he said, 1.35.

LILY: It's the railway's fault, not ours.

GUARD: Your leaflet's got nothing to do with it. Gateway to the heartland of the English Lakes! It's not even a British Rail leaflet. Now are you going . . . Just a minute.

*The train is slowing down.*

Unless you want to get off here, in which case, you can pay at the barrier.

LILY: Get knotted!

GUARD: I'll be back!

*Door slides back. Footsteps. The train slows to a halt. More footsteps, doors banging, etc.*

LILY: Quick, Colin.

COLIN: They'll catch us at the barrier; there's no hope.

LILY: We'll hide in t'toilet until the next station. Come on.

*We hear them pack up quickly. The door slides back, footsteps.*

Not this toilet, the next one down.

*More footsteps, toilet door opens and closes, latch clicks.*
*(Inside toilet)*   Don't lock it, leave it vacant, then he won't
suspect.

*The whistle blows. The train moves off.*

COLIN:   It's a terrible risk.

LILY:   Shhh!

*Guard's footsteps. Door slides. Pause. Footsteps retreating.*
*The train gathers speed.*

LILY:   *(a loud whisper)*   When we get to t'next station, we'll
jump off and run into t'waiting-room and stay there for a
bit. Then we'll saunter out, as if nothing had happened.

*Pause.*

If you sit on the toilet, I'll sit on your knee, Colin. It's a
bit cramped wi' both of us standing.

COLIN:   You sit on the toilet and I'll stand. I prefer to stand.

*Pause. The train noises are slightly louder than before, now*
*that they are in the toilet.*

It's a sign, Lily. Jesus Christ is beckoning us. This isn't the
wrong train at all, this is the train that Jesus Christ, Our
Lord indicated to us. That guard was an angel of the devil,
sent to pursue us, but Our Lord said to us, go ye into the
toilet and find shelter.

LILY:   D'you reckon?

COLIN:   I know. The Lord is on our side.

*Pause.*

LILY:   If it was cleaned up a bit, it'd be a very nice toilet; fit for
anybody, fit for a lord. If we get a caravan, Colin, I hope
there's a toilet just like this.

*Pause.*

Do you think if we rented a caravan, the council would help us to buy it?

COLIN:   I doubt it.

LILY:   They help people to buy their houses. There's a family on our estate buying theirs.

COLIN:   I've never aspired to a council house. A room of my own in a lodging house, not having to share, that's the most I've ever hoped for.

LILY:   One day we'll have our own caravan, and not on a big site either, a small site.

COLIN:   Select.

LILY:   Yeah.

*Brief fade. Then we hear the train clattering over points and beginning to slow.*

LILY:   Jesus is beckoning again, Colin. He says, don't get off the minute t'train stops, wait till it's nearly ready to go, then jump off quick, otherwise the guard'll get us. You ready?

*The train stops, doors open. The toilet door opens. Footsteps. Door clicks. Other doors slam. Whistle goes.*

Ready!

*We hear LILY and COLIN jump down and a door slam behind them. There is an angry shout, deafened by the noise of the train pulling out.*

*Fade out.*

*Time passes – i.e. overnight. Music to indicate fading into country noises – sheep baa-ing, etc., then loud clear bird-song of early morning. Rustling of straw.*

LILY:  *(drowsily)*  Colin . . . Colin . . . Colin! Where are you? My love . . . I couldn't see you.

COLIN:  I was watching you while you slept.

LILY:  Lovingly?

COLIN:  I was watching you lovingly. I've never watched anyone asleep before, at least, not a young lady.

LILY:  Like a prince, watching his princess.

COLIN:  Your eyelashes were very long against your cheeks and your mouth was slightly open.

LILY:  Was I snoring?

COLIN:  Not that I was aware.

*Pause. Straw rustles.*

LILY:  I slept like a princess, all night long, under the straw. Just think, Colin. If me dad hadn't beaten me up and I hadn't run away and your landlady hadn't taken me in, I'd never have met you and I'd never be here now. This is going to be the happiest day of my life.

COLIN:  I've never met anyone like you, Lily.

LILY:  And I've never met anyone like you.

*Pause. A bird sings loudly.*

The English Lakes . . .

COLIN:  Lovely Lake Windermere, Wordsworth's Cottage . . .

LILY:  Wi' roses round the door and chubby-cheeked children. Do you think God can see our happiness, Colin?

COLIN:  God sees everything.

LILY:  We must be like two specks from up there.

COLIN:  He sees the good things in us, and he sees what's evil and wrong.

LILY:   I bet he's seeing good at the moment.

COLIN:   Oh, he is.

LILY:   Me, I'm bursting wi' goodness.

*Pause. Country noises.*

Do you wish this moment would last for ever? You and me in the English Lake District?

COLIN:   My whole life is made of moments, if the truth be told, with long grey patches in between. Good and bad moments, mostly bad.

LILY:   Don't say it, Colin! This is a good moment.

COLIN:   Because of you, Lily. You've done a lot for me. You raised me up when I was low. You comforted me in my hour of need.

LILY:   I'm so happy, Colin, so happy. I could live here for ever in the morning dew. But I won't, because I'm starving.

*Rustling of straw as she gets up.*

Will you dust me down?

*We hear* COLIN *doing so.*

COLIN:   You've got it all over you. Turn round.

LILY:   What are we going to do about our breakfast?

COLIN:   The Lord will provide.

LILY:   He might show us a milk bottle to nick on somebody's doorstep, or one at a farm.

COLIN:   I'm sure he'll put something in our way. Shall we depart?

LILY:   I've never slept in a barn before. Ta, ta, comfortable barn.

*Footsteps, as they walk away. Brief fade.*

*Country noises and footsteps as they continue walking.*

LILY:   The English Lakes, the English Lakes . . . I can't actually
see an English lake. Do you think if we keep on walking
we'll see one?

COLIN:   They'll show the English Lakes on the souvenirs. You
can see one on an ashtray or an egg-cup.

LILY:   As soon as we get to a town we'll go straight to the
souvenir shop. Then we'll have some dinner. Then we'll
have a lovely time.

*They continue walking. Fade out.*

*Police station noises in background.*

FATHER:   I didn't want kids in t'first place but she never did owt
about it, so what do you expect? Then she died, didn't she,
when our Lily was three. She were coughing. I knew she
weren't right like, but then she smoked, we're both heavy
smokers. I thought it were just t'fags making her cough. I
told her to lay off, but she wouldn't. T'doctor said it were
bronchitis, but by then it were too late, t'damage had been
done and she were dead by t'end of t'week.
I give her a good funeral. You can say what you like, but I
give her a bloody good send-off – set me back for months
it did.
   Life weren't easy. I had the two kiddies to bring up and
I had to do as much overtime as I could, to pay for
t'funeral. Our Nancy were at school and that's when our
Lily started going round to her nan's. Now, could I be at
home wi' her? Of course, since I were laid off, it's
different. I'm home all t' bloody time now and that gets on
me nerves more than ever t'overtime did.
I blame her nan – she's dead now, died three year ago when
our Lily was ten. She were a bad influence. Since she died,
I can't do owt wi' Lily. She won't bloody communicate,
for a start. You can ask her a question – she won't answer;

you can shout at her, you can slap her – I have hit her, I
admit it. Not hard like, I don't believe in hitting women,
but she can make you that mad. I've had t'school round,
I've had t'police round, I've had Welfare round and they
all say t'same thing – they can't do owt wi' her. So what
they expect me to do, God knows; I'm no bloody expert.
I'm no child psychologist. They're paid to do it, they can
bloody sort her out. I want a bit of peace. She's a thieving
little bitch – ten pounds she took off me before she went,
and she took her sister's cassette recorder which isn't paid
for, so that's more trouble.
Lily's the name, Lily Porter, age thirteen, missing since
yesterday breakfast time. I want her found and I want her
put away. I can't cope any more.

*Shop door pings as* LILY *and* COLIN *walk in.*

SHOPWOMAN:  Are you the coach party?

COLIN:  We've come looking for souvenirs.

LILY:  We walked for miles and miles to get here.

SHOPWOMAN:  Morning coffee at the Copper Kettle, they told
me, and then coming here straight after. I've seen no sign
of them and it's gone half-past twelve. I've called in extra
help as well.

LILY:  Can we look round?

SHOPWOMAN:  Do what you like, dear, the prices should all be
marked. I know what'll happen, they'll come in just as I'm
popping out for lunch. I'll put some music on for you,
liven the place up a bit.

*Canned music.* LILY *and* COLIN *walk round the shop.*

(calls out)  Very attractive, aren't they, those mugs? I've
not had them in for long, but they're very popular.

LILY:  *(whispers to* COLIN*)*  They always tell you the expensive
things.

COLIN:   The handles come off mugs and you can never stop other people using them. I'm thinking more of an ashtray or a set of egg-cups. These are nice, a different lake on each one.

LILY:   'Tea', 'coffee', 'sugar', how about these? Or those wooden spoons, they're alright, wi' a lake painted on the spoon and a tassle on the handle. You wouldn't have to use them, but they're nice.

COLIN:   How much?

LILY:   Er . . . £1.75. It is a bit much.

COLIN:   The egg-cups are £3.60.

SHOPWOMAN   *(calls out)*   Will you tell your father not to touch, dear, if he doesn't mind. Things mark so easily, don't they?

LILY:   How are we meant to see the prices, then?

SHOPWOMAN:   You can always ask.

LILY:   They're expensive prices.

SHOPWOMAN:   It depends what you're looking for. Your dinner hour is it, dear?

LILY:   No, it's not. And he's not my father, he's my lover.

*They go on round the shop.*

COLIN:   *(whispers)*   She's one of them, Lily. I don't trust her. Let's go, before something happens.

LILY:   Hang on a minute.

*The shop bell pins. There is a buzz of voices.*

SHOPWOMAN:   What did I tell you!

VOICES:   Held up two hours . . . nice cup of coffee . . . half an hour . . . not long . . . just have a look at this . . . beautiful.

SHOPWOMAN:   The prices should all be marked . . .

LILY   *(whispers over the buzz of voices)*   Open your carrier, Colin.

COLIN:   No, Lily! She'll see us!

LILY:   Quick!

COLIN:   Take that set of plates, then – Coniston, Windermere and Derwentwater.

*Buzz of voices.*

SHOPWOMAN:   *(in background)*   The mugs are very attractive. I've not had them in for long, but they're proving very popular.   *(To* LILY *and* COLIN*)*   You didn't find anything, then?

LILY:   No.

SHOPWOMAN:   Very good.

*Shop door pings. Street noises as* LILY *and* COLIN *go outside.*

COLIN:   The Lord is on our side, Lily. He sees us, His humble servants and He says, 'I will provide'. In His goodness, He delayed that coach party. Trust in the Lord, Lily, and all will be well.

*Brief fade.*

LILY:   I'm hungry again. Look out for a supermarket.

*Street noises, cars driving past, etc.*

I've always nicked from supermarkets. I've been caught only once, by the shopwalker. She were just a lass wi' army trousers on and a green jumper. Just a normal lass that you'd never notice. But she nicked me.

COLIN:   There's a Boots the Chemists.

LILY:   Boots is where it happened. I'd just come on and I'd no money at all, so I went to get some sani towels. The one time I really had to thieve and I must have got careless, but when it happens to you unexpected . . .

COLIN:  I don't like this kind of talk, Lily.

LILY:  It's a fact of life. You can't run away from facts.

COLIN:  Even so . . . no, you're right. You are right.

LILY:  I wouldn't talk dirty, Colin, I wouldn't. I've had enough of that.

COLIN:  Oh, I do so agree with you.

*They walk on.*

LILY:  Woolies! Hurray! You said the Lord would provide and sure enough, there's Woolies. I know me way round Woolies. Let's cross.

*Street noises as they cross the road.*

Now, you wait for me here, Colin, only don't look as if you're waiting. Look like a passer-by, wi' money in yer pocket.

COLIN:  I'll put an inconspicuous look on my face.

LILY:  And when I come out, don't rush up. Just pass on by and catch me up as you go.

COLIN:  Don't make me nervous.

LILY:  I'm not.

COLIN:  I can't look inconspicuous with my heart in my mouth.

LILY:  Vision Hire. Here you are. Bananaman in four different sizes. I won't be long. Trust me.

*A gust of supermarket music as Woolworth's door opens. Brief fade.*

LILY:  Psst! Don't look round.

*Running footsteps.*

COLIN:  Don't go so fast.

LILY:  Keep going.

*Brief fade.*

LILY:  This'll do nicely. There were a fella in there who I didn't like the look of. Normally, it's best not to run.

COLIN:  I should think we're safe in a car park.

LILY *rustles in the carrier bag.*

LILY:  Two strawberry mousses, an angel cake – it said, 'on offer', so I thought that must be meant for us – a packet of Sunblest, a packet of crisps (prawn cocktail) and a bottle of tomato sauce. Alright, eh! And I've still got them tins I brought from home, but I'll have to nick a tin opener before we can have them.

COLIN:  Pass me a slice of bread, please.

LILY:  I always liked sauce butties. I used to have 'em for a treat at me nana's. Hold yer bread out and I'll put a dollop on for you.

*Pause while they eat. Footsteps across gravel of car park.*

ADA:  Can we get out this way, or have we to go round?

EDIE:  We'll cut through, Ada.

ADA:  Litter. I've not seen anything like it.

EDIE:  You get all sorts, dear, you can't stop it.

ADA:  You can stop them.

EDIE:  Mind how you go.

ADA:  Our own nationals! They're worse than the foreign ones.

*Their voices fade into the distance.*

COLIN:   A lot of superficial types judge others by their appearance.

LILY:   I bet they didn't know what to make of us. That shop woman thought you were me dad!

COLIN:   God knows what we truly are. He knows that our souls are pure, in spite of external appearances.

LILY:   God doesn't worry about your plimsolls or your orange shirt.

COLIN:   I got it from the WVS women. It was either this or a T-shirt with Cambridge University on it. I selected the orange; I though it was more appropriate.

LILY:   God doesn't worry, and I don't worry either. And I like you being older. I can't stand lads of me own age, they're daft. I look at you and I think, he's had all that experience of life, he's seen so much and he's done so much and he's still chosen me. Have some more bread.

COLIN:   I've already had four slices.

LILY:   I never thought to get any margarine.

*Pause while they eat. Car park noises in background.*

COLIN:   I've often had trouble with my appearance in the past.

LILY:   And I have.  *(Mimics)*   You look nice, Lily, have you washed your hair? I don't bother to say anything. I just think to mesel', you stupid git!

COLIN:   My aunty – the one I had to call aunty – she made me wear short trousers when all the other boys were wearing long. My legs grew very long and white, and even when I did acquire some full-length trousers, they were too short. Her Melvin's were always the correct length.

LILY:   How you must have suffered.

COLIN:   I used to look at myself in the mirror and think, no
wonder your mother didn't want to keep you, an ugly
looking thing like you. It was only when I discovered the
Lord that my appearance ceased to worry me.

*Pause for eating.*

LILY:   We can keep t'rest of bread for later and there's some
sauce left too.

COLIN:   It's nice sauce, very appetising. In most of the lodgings
where I've resided, the landlords buy it in bulk – catering
sauce, catering margarine – but they buy proper bottles for
themselves and margarine in tubs, or even butter. Very
rarely is it the same for everybody. If we even do have our
own place, I intend to have HP and decent Stork. We'll
start off as we mean to go on.

LILY:   And mugs without chips in them.

COLIN:   With handles, though. And souvenir mugs for special
occasions.

LILY:   Have some angel cake.

COLIN:   I will, thank you.

LILY:   It's crumbly.

COLIN:   I like the crumbly bits.

*Pause while they eat.*

LILY:   Posh, eh? Angel cake!

COLIN:   I prefer Swiss Roll, chocolate with cream. This is very
appetising, though.

*Pause.*

It's nice having you to talk to, Lily. I've never felt I could
really converse with anyone before, and not for want of
subject matter, either. Take my souvenirs, for instance –

my egg-cup from the Isle of Man, my ashtray from Bristol Zoo and the rest. They're very interesting. I've often wanted to show them to people, but I know they'd only laugh. You're different.

LILY:   There's your interest in religion too, Colin.

COLIN:   And the various religious experiences I've had.

LILY:   And the history you know.

COLIN:   Exactly. And I've not even started in my dreams yet.

*Pub noises in background – voices, laughter, clinking glasses, etc.*

*Suitable background as* MR WRIGHT *takes his change and goes to a table.*

MR WRIGHT:   They didn't have any cheese and onion.

MISS SMART:   That's alright. Cheers!

MR WRIGHT:   We had the police in school this morning, checking up on one of your clients.

MISS SMART:   Doesn't surprise me. Which one?

MR WRIGHT:   Lily Porter.

MISS SMART:   What's Lily been up to?

MR WRIGHT:   She hasn't been at school for the last few days. The police think she might have gone off with some man.

MISS SMART:   Oh no! Oh no!

MR WRIGHT:   They were going to contact you.

MISS SMART:   I've been in court all morning. Oh God, who is this man?

MR WRIGHT:   They didn't say. He's a lot older than Lily. They don't know whether he's forced her to go with him or whether she's chosen to go.

MISS SMART:    Dammit. I thought everything was going alright
with her. Little pest.    *(Sighs with annoyance.)*    I'm going
to get the chop over Lily if I'm not careful.

MR WRIGHT:    I'm sure she's probably alright. It's difficult to see
what sort of older man would go for her.

MISS SMART:    My boss wanted to put her in care some time ago.
She's a great believer in tidying cases up, and it was me that
said no, I didn't think it would do Lily any good. Damn! If
this man has abducted Lily in some way, there's going to
be a hell of a row. The police didn't give you any more
idea?

MR WRIGHT:    His name's Colin and he's a lot older than her.
He's been in prison several times but apparently has no
record of messing with little girls.

MISS SMART:    That's something. Who was the policeman?

MR WRIGHT:    Inspector Pye.

MISS SMART:    I'll get onto him.

MR WRIGHT:    He wanted to know about her background but he
didn't seem too worried once I'd told him.

MISS SMART:    I'm worried! Older man, thirteen-year-old girl,
social worker's responsibility. You know how these things
can go. How do you find Lily?

MR WRIGHT:    Insignificant, withdrawn, a bit of a tough nut on
the quiet. Not very bright, but could do better if she tried
harder . . . that's about it.

MISS SMART:    She's got an appalling father, of course. I just hope
they pick her up as soon as possible and I can advise the
magistrate to slap a care order on her. I don't suppose it'll
do much for her, but it should keep her out of the clutches
of older men, God help us. He must be some sort of nut.

MR WRIGHT:   Must be. What a thought! What have they got today? Steak and kidney pie – that'll do. Are you having lunch?

MISS SMART:   I'll have to get back – see what I can dig out on Lily.

*Music for the time passing, which fades into rain falling.*

COLIN:   The birds have their nests and the foxes have their dens but the Son of Man wanders alone in the wilderness without home or shelter.

LILY:   But we could try the church.

COLIN:   Let's run.

*We hear them running through the rain up the flagged walk and into the church porch.* LILY *twists and turns the handle of the door.*

LILY:   It's locked, Colin. God's house is locked!

COLIN *kicks the door.*

It's no good.

LILY *sighs. The rain falls outside and on the porch roof above them.*

LILY:   Was it nice and sunny in the wilderness, or did the son of man suffer wind and rain like us?

COLIN:   Oh, it was hot and sunny – desert.

LILY:   He was lucky, then – in a way.

*Rain noises.*

COLIN:   Are you suffering, Lily?

LILY:   I didn't think to bring a coat. Daft, eh? I just walked out and I never thought of anything except, now I'm free for ever. It would have been better if I'd brought a coat.

COLIN: If we could find a way into the church, you could wrap the vicar's robes around you. I can't speak for the vicar, but I'm certain Our Lord wouldn't mind.

*They try the handle again.*

Poor little Lily, you're soaked. My jacket's wet but you can have it. Here. It's only blue denim but it's better than nothing.

LILY: Oh Colin . . . oh Colin . . .

COLIN: Don't upset yourself.

LILY: You're so kind and gentle wi' me. God wouldn't lock this house, would he, if it was left to him?

COLIN: It's the devil at work again, that's very plain.

LILY: Maybe God's in there, calling out to us, come in Colin and Lily, come in, out of the rain.

COLIN: Well, I suggest we put our names on the door. Our Lord God will know the reason, he'll see it's a sign unto him, that we were here. I've got a penknife in my pocket.

LILY: Put 'Colin loves Lily'.

COLIN: I will.

*Scratching of penknife on wood.*

The wood is very old and hard. 'COLIN loves LI . . .'

LILY It'll be there for all to see.

COLIN: Showing up nicely.

LILY: It's lovely.

*Pause. More rain noises.*

Still raining.

*Rustling in carrier bag.*

T'bread's got wet. Hope the cassette recorder's alright.

COLIN:    Of course, there's always his reverence.

LILY:    Who's that?

COLIN:    I daresay he lives in that house over there. Can you see, behind the trees?

LILY:    Will he let us stay the night?

COLIN:    Not in his house he won't, they never do that. They unlock sheds for you, though, or occasionally a church hall – it depends.

LILY:    What is a 'reverence'?

COLIN:    A holy man of God.

LILY:    We don't have them round our way.

COLIN:    I have my doubts about them. In my opinion, some of them aren't men of God at all. In fact, I know they're not. I've spotted certain signs that give them away, signs that the ordinary run of person wouldn't notice. But then, the ordinary run of person isn't God-fearing at all, let's face it.

LILY:    What shall we say to him, Colin?

COLIN:    We'll knock on his door and we'll say we're two travellers of no fixed abode, and we've come to throw ourselves on his mercy and to beg in the name of the Lord for a shelter over our heads during the hours of darkness.

LILY:    We'll say we want a room for the night wi' a nice bed and clean sheets. Come on, the rain's slacking off.

*Fade out.*

*A house doorbell rings, followed by knocking. Pop music comes out of the cassette recorder. Voice inside house, 'They've come! They're here! Will you go to the door!'.*

*The door opens.*

VICAR:    Come on in! Ah . . .

VICAR'S WIFE:  *(calling from inside)*  Come in, come in!

VICAR:  *(calls back into house)*  Just a minute, dear.  *(To* LILY *and* COLIN*)*  Very jolly!

COLIN:  We hungered and thirsted . . .

LILY:  We want a bed for the night.

VICAR:  I said, that sounds very jolly.

LILY:  We went to the church. It were locked.

VICAR:  Coming to call with music in your hands! Personally, my choice is rather more conservative. But you'll have to turn it down if you want me to hear what you're saying. Preferably off – but down will do.

*Music off.*

Ooh . . . quiet! Good evening. What can I do for you? How can I help you?

COLIN:  Your reverence, we are humble travellers . . .

LILY:  Give us a bed. We won't mess it. We'll be gone in t'morning.

VICAR:  Ah ha.

*Pause.*

Come in, travellers. Come in.

*They go into the house.*

*(calls)*  Darling, I'm taking our friends here through to the kitchen.

*They walk through the house.*

Grab a pew. I'll put the kettle on.

LILY:  Is this your kitchen?

VICAR:  It is.

*Water runs for kettle.*

LILY:   It's dead posh.

VICAR:   Thank you kindly.

COLIN:   Are you acquainted with Reverend Arthur Philpott?

VICAR:   Philpott? Do you know, I don't think I am. Has he a parish in this area?

COLIN:   I was his friend. We were intimate friends.

*Panting and general dog noises.*

LILY:   Ah! No! Get off!

VICAR:   Bose! He's a friendly sort of chap. Just push him away.

LILY:   Colin!

VICAR:   Bose! Come away!

LILY:   I hate dogs.

COLIN:   It's alright, Lily. Get down, you slavering brute! Get down!

VICAR:   Lie down, Bose, good boy. He wants to play with you.

LILY:   He had his teeth at me.

VICAR:   He loves to play. Cup of tea?

LILY:   Yeah!

VICAR:   The enthusiasm of youth, eh! Let me see, you must be . . . er . . .

LILY:   We're lovers.

COLIN:   Lily and I love each other.

*Tea pouring.*

VICAR:   Excuse me if I don't join you in the tea round. But yes, do smoke.

*Matches striking, etc.*

LILY:  Is there any sugar?

VICAR:  Only brown, I'm afraid.

LILY:  Is it alright to put it in?

VICAR:  Quite alright. So, good people . . . tell me . . .

COLIN:  The Reverend Arthur Philpott invited me into his kitchen – he was always very civil. He asked me to call him Arthur, that's how intimate we were. I'm surprised you're not acquainted with him.

VICAR:  Stay, Bose, stay.

COLIN:  I hope you won't take it as a liberty if I say I think this is a lovely kitchen. In fact, your reverence, in my opinion, you have a lovely home, if you'll pardon the liberty.

VICAR:  You want to go outside, do you? No? Then lie down. Lie. What a baby. You will be needing an ashtray any minute now, my dear, so if you hold it. Just a tick. There we are.

LILY:  Can I have some more of your sugar?

VICAR:  You can indeed.

COLIN:  And I'd also like to comment on the tea. It's very nice tea. It's not often I partake of such nice tea.

VICAR:  Have some more.

COLIN:  One cup will suffice, but I assure you . . .

LILY:  Colin!

COLIN:  It's alright, Lily. I'm enjoying conversing with his reverence.

LILY:  Will you let us stay?

*The telephone rings.*

VICAR: Momento. *(Into phone)* Hello . . . thought it might be you . . . No, no . . . left at the filling station, then we're on the right. You can't miss the church . . . jolly good . . . we're all looking forward to it . . . I'll tell them . . . See you in a minute . . . Bye.

LILY: Will you?

VICAR: I'm sorry?

LILY: Will you let us stop the night?

VICAR: Ah ha!

LILY: We'll be gone in t'morning.

COLIN: It goes without saying, your reverence, that we'll do something in return for your hospitality. You won't find us wanting in that respect.

LILY: Let us stay.

*Pause.*

VICAR: Oh my golly gosh!

LILY: You're a reverence, aren't you? You're meant to be better than other people. You ought to have a kennel or a shed you could let us have. It's raining out there.

VICAR: Dear good people, I would so love to help you. But, do you know, I rather think you'd be better off at home.

LILY: We haven't got a home.

VICAR: Don't tell me that your mother and father aren't worried about you.

LILY: My mum's dead.

VICAR: I'm so sorry.

*Pause.*

LILY: Let us stay.

VICAR:   Your father . . .

LILY:   What about him?

VICAR:   He must be concerned.

LILY:   He hates me and I hate him.

VICAR:   Take her back home.

LILY:   You're not going to help us, are you?

VICAR:   Dear girl, I *am* helping you, I'm telling you to go home
– back to your family. In their way, they love you, I'm
sure of it.

COLIN:   There's washing-up in the sink. I'll make a start. You
won't find me wanting in gratitude.

*He stands up.*

VICAR:   No, no . . . please . . .

*Sound of water running into bowl.*

LILY:   How can you know them? My dad'd smash your face in
after he'd had a few drinks.

VICAR:   Please leave the washing-up.

*Clattering dishes.*

COLIN:   I'm a rapid worker, once I get going.

VICAR:   Leave the dishes.

LILY:   He's only trying to help.

VICAR:   Leave them!

COLIN:   *(still clattering)*   If there's a tea-towel, I'll do the
drying as well. I had a position once, washing-up.

VICAR:   I must ask you to go. I must ask you to take her home.

LILY:   I'm not going home.

VICAR:   Will you give me your word?

LILY:   He's helping you.

VICAR:   Otherwise, I shall have to take steps.

COLIN:   Hand me a tea-towel.

VICAR:   No.

LILY:   There's one on t'rail there, Colin.

VICAR:   Put that tea-towel down.

COLIN:   I wish to help.

VICAR:   I don't want your help. I want you to go.

LILY:   We won't.

*The dog growls.*

COLIN:   You're spurning us, aren't you?

VICAR:   I wish I could help you, I wish you well, if you want me to ring the Samaritans, I will, but I'm asking you to go now.

LILY:   No.

*The dog growls again.*

COLIN:   I don't like being spurned. I go funny when I'm spurned.

*The VICAR pushes his chair back.*

VICAR:   Out!

*Footsteps as they retreat.*

COLIN:   Something might happen to you; something you won't like.

VICAR:   I don't respond to threats.

LILY:   Give us some money and we'll go away.

VICAR:  Goodnight.

COLIN:  If something happens, I won't be responsible. I get very angry, I can't help it. You've brought the wrath of God upon yourself.

*The door shuts firmly.*

LILY:  *(shouting)*  It's wet out here. Mean sod!

COLIN:  I'll do something! I'll do it! God help me, I will!

LILY:  Smash his windows.

*We hear their feet on the gravel of the drive.*

COLIN:  The tin of peaches, that'll do.

*Pause. Then a crash and loud smashing of glass.*

LILY:  Tin of milk!

*Another smash. Angry shouting.*

COLIN:  Lake Windermere!

*Another smash of glass. A car turns in.*

LILY:  There's his friends. Let's run.

*Running footsteps.*

They're coming! They'll stop us!

*The car screeches to a halt.*

COLIN:  This way! Round the side! Run! Oh, Lily, run!

*The car door slams. Angry voices shouting. Panting breath.*

LILY:  In here.

*A door unlatches and then closes again.*

COLIN:  *(panting, inside shed)*  What is it?

LILY:  *(panting)*  Can't see much. Yes, I can. There's a fork and a shovel and some pots.

COLIN:   And there's wood stacked up at the end.

LILY:   It's quite big. There's plenty of room. What a liar! He said he couldn't let us have a shed.

COLIN:   He deserved what happened.

LILY:   We could have smashed more windows if that car hadn't come.

COLIN:   I could have gone a lot further. He's lucky I restrained myself.

LILY:   You could have thrown Lake Coniston and Lake Derwentwater, as well.

COLIN:   Oh God! Did I throw one of my souvenir plates,–did I?

LILY:   Lake Windermere.

COLIN:   So many of my things have been smashed or stolen. It wasn't my fault, Lily.

LILY:   It was the reverend's fault. Of course it was.

*Pause.*

D'you reckon he'll come looking for us?

COLIN:   I won't be responsible for what happens if he does.

*We hear* LILY *scrambling up to look out of the window.*

LILY:   Can't see anyone. Why don't we stop here? Why don't we get a fire going, warm oursel's up a bit? There's a stack of paper in the corner, and there's the wood.

COLIN:   I have got a problem, I know that. It's been said to me often enough. They told me that's why my mother couldn't keep me – because I was a problem. I don't remember her myself. Then my aunty, you know who I mean, she said the same – Colin's got a problem. That's why I was sent to this school, Kingsdown School for Boys – not a pleasant place. They suggested I should join the army, but when I went to the examination, I was found unfit and that was because of my problems.

LILY:   You might have been a soldier, Colin.

COLIN:   After many years, I realised it was the wrath of God speaking through me. God knows best.

LILY:   It's getting real dark.   *(Reading out)*   'Save T R I . . . dent', 'Save Trident'. 'Vote Conservative'. They're just a pile of old posters.

*Paper being screwed up.*

Me nana showed me how to make a fire. Up against the side. Pass some of that wood.

*Fire-making preparation.*

I'll screw up two or three.

*A match strikes.*

And the wood.

*Fire crackles.*

COLIN:   But I can't cease worrying. I know I should. I get so het up. Look at me, I'm still shaking.   *(He coughs.)*

LILY:   Poor Colin.   *(She coughs.)*

COLIN:   It's very smoky.

LILY:   There's no chimbley, that's why. Can you feel it warm?

*More coughing.*

Them posters were damp. If there'd been a chimbley, it would be all right.

*Fit of coughing.*

COLIN:   My eyes! I can't see! This isn't for us, Lily. Let's go, it's stopped raining.

LILY: It's blazing up now. *(She coughs.)*

COLIN: Come on!

LILY: This bloody smoke!

*The door bursts open. They gasp for breath.*

LILY: Not past the house. We'll go round back of t'shed.

COLIN: The fire's going well now, you can see the flames.

LILY: What if it burns his shed down? *(She giggles.)* He'll wish he'd given us a room for t' night.

COLIN: It's the wrath of God. We've done nothing, nothing. We'll go over the fence, then we can get back to the road.

LILY: We could have stayed in that shed. We could have made it nice and homelike. Now it's no use to anybody. Maybe it's too wet to burn right down, but we could have had a nice little home there. Now we have to go to t' bus station, and if it's owt like t' bus station at home, it'll be cold and horrible wi' nasty old men around and drunks.

COLIN: We'll go to the railway station. I much prefer trains. Come on, Lily, let's get out of here.

*Roaring of fire. Police/fire siren to full blast, then fade out.*

VICAR: They came out of the blue, threatened me, broke the windows in the living-room, bedroom and study, as you can see. Fortunately, our visitors arrived and they ran. I went over to the church because they mentioned they'd been there and found they had desecrated our fourteenth-century church door. I came home to find the shed was blazing. The girl will be fourteen at the most, the man over thirty-five. We've never had this sort of thing before. For all our sakes, find them soon.

*Night noises. An owl hoots, siren faint in the distance. Hurried footsteps.*

LILY: They're bound to be looking for us, but I don't care. They can't destroy our love, can they?

COLIN: Keep walking, Lily.

*They carry on walking.*

LILY: I'm tired, Colin.

COLIN: We mustn't stop.

LILY: I've still got that ten pound note. Maybe we could go for a bed and breakfast.

COLIN: Think of the questions they'd ask. Father and daughter? Where have you been? Where're you from?

LILY: Why're you so scruffy looking?

COLIN: No . . . no . . . I'm upset enough as it is.

*A train is heard in the distance.*

COLIN: It's not far to the railway station.

*They carry on walking.*

We'll have to leave the English Lake District. Anything can happen once I get upset.

LILY: Where will we go?

COLIN: Don't ask . . . don't ask.

LILY: The Scottish Highlands?

COLIN: Just keep walking.

*They walk on.*

LILY: British Rail. It's a tiny station.

COLIN: All the better.

*Footsteps approach.*

GUARD: It's gone. You've missed it. T'last train's just gone. Missed it by five minutes.

LILY:   Can we stop on t'station?

GUARD:   For the night, do you mean?

LILY:   We've got to stop somewhere.

GUARD:   I don't know about that. I'll have to think about that one.

*Pause.*

You've come to the right person, I will say. Last night you wouldn't have had a hope, not with Joe Jarvis. I do lates, Wednesdays. You're in luck, as it happens.

LILY:   We only want somewhere to sit for t'night. We'll do no harm.

GUARD:   Who's he, your dad?

LILY:   We're lovers.

GUARD:   I thought there was more to it. Runaway love, eh? The sort you read about in the paper, I see . . . There again, you've hit lucky. Me, I'm very broad-minded.

COLIN:   A lot of people make judgements.

GUARD:   Not me, squire. Live and let live, I say. I tell you what – it takes me a few minutes to lock up – you sit in the waiting-room and I'll think it over. No promises mind – but you never know, you just might have caught me in a good mood, you just might.

*Brief fade.*

*In waiting room.*

LILY:   I'm so tired, I could sleep 'til next week. That's what me nana used to say. I do hope he lets us stay.

COLIN:   What have I got you into, Lily?

LILY:   That's no way to talk.

COLIN:   I've dragged you away from home, exposed you to evil influences . . .

LILY:   Where you are, there's my home. That barn last night, tonight this is our home, we hope, and tomorrow night, who knows? I don't care, Colin, as long as I'm with you.

COLIN:   I'm not worthy. I never have been. I've had friends before – not like you, not lovers – but kindly people have taken an interest in me from time to time. The Reverend Arthur Philpott, for one, and I've always betrayed their trust.
I'll tell you now, Lily, that was a lie. Reverend Arthur wasn't my intimate friend at all and I didn't call him Arthur, either. He was kind to me, he trusted me and I let him down. He said he was very sorry but there was no possibility of him trusting me again.

LILY:   I tell lies all t'time. Not to you, my love, but to everyone else. There's no point in telling t'truth, it only gets you into trouble. You've got to tell lies to help yourself.

COLIN:   He was the prison chaplain, that's where I met him. I didn't tell you I'd been to prison. And not once, several times.

LILY:   I know that.

COLIN:   I'm a cheat and a liar, Lily.

LILY:   And I am.

COLIN:   I can see no reason for anyone to concern themselves with me.

LILY:   Then you're daft.

*The door opens.*

GUARD:   I've been thinking.

LILY:   Will you let us stay?

GUARD: I didn't say I'd reached a conclusion, did I? Got you there. I just said, I'm thinking, and I'm still thinking.

LILY: It's nice here.

GUARD: Ah ha! You won't get round me that way. It is nice. I happen to think it's one of the nicest station waiting-rooms in the country. That is my personal opinion. But I'm not going to let that make any difference.

*Pause.*

I'm just going to lock the boiler room, then I'll be back with my considered opinion.

*The door closes behind him.*

COLIN: Go home, Lily, for God's sake.

LILY: No.

COLIN: Don't expect me to have anything to do with you. I intend to ignore you.

LILY: I'll make you notice me. I'll jump up and down, I'll sing to you.

COLIN: In the morning, you'll get the first train back home.

LILY: I won't.

COLIN: I'll go to Barrow, to the night shelter. I daresay the probation service can fix me up with accommodation and, if not, I can always return to prison.

LILY: You're trying to upset me, I know you are. Well, I won't be upset.

COLIN: I don't want you hanging on to me. I'm not up to it.

LILY: Don't say it.

COLIN: I'll say what I like.

LILY: I'm not upset, I'm not.

COLIN:   You're making yourself ridiculous.

LILY:   You are.

COLIN:   You are. You're young, you're ridiculous, you're . . .

*His words are drowned by a heavy-goods train pounding through. As the noise dies away, the waiting-room door opens.*

GUARD:   Did you hear that?

LILY:   Course.

GUARD:   Did you see it?

LILY:   Suppose so . . . Yeah.

GUARD:   Well, I'm telling you, you didn't hear it and you didn't see it.

LILY:   What're you on about?

GUARD:   Nothing! I'm on about nothing, because there was nothing, right!

*Pause.*

Do you know what was on that non-existent train? I'm not telling you, but if you were one of those CND people or one of those anti-nuclear people, you'd be very interested, very interested indeed. That's why it's non-existent, top secret. You look on any of the schedules and you won't see it.

LILY:   Will you let us stay?

GUARD:   How do I know you're not spies? Answer me that one? They get all sorts to support them, do these peace people. Some of our lads here even, they're in with them. But then, they don't work nights and I do, and I know when to keep my mouth shut.

COLIN:   It's the responsibility.

GUARD:   Thank you, squire, that's just it. It is the
responsibility. Mind you, I support nuclear weapons, I'm
all for them. The way I look at it, those train loads going
through, they're protection.

COLIN:   Responsibility . . . responsibility . . . it's a very serious
thing. Being responsible for yourself is enough for anyone.

GUARD:   Think of Maggie, think what she's responsible for. A
lot of the lads here don't see it, but the way I look at it,
she's responsible for everything. There's been a hospital
and a school closed in the town and the railway's bound to
close for passengers, bound to – which means most of our
jobs 'll go – and Maggie's responsible for it all. I couldn't
take that on, no way. They don't see it, though. I say to
them, could you do that, take all the aggro, like she does?
Maggie knows about these secret trains, but does she let
on? Course she doesn't.

LILY:   We won't let on if you let us stay.

GUARD:   *(laughs)*   Don't say you could do better than Maggie
Thatcher, because I just won't believe you.

LILY:   Even she's got to sleep. That's all we want to do, sleep
here.

*Pause.*

GUARD:   Alright then. Go on. I shouldn't, but I will. No hanky
panky, mind. I don't want to read about you in the Sunday
papers.

LILY:   We'll be gone in t' morning.

COLIN:   The birds have their nests and the foxes have their dens,
but the son of man wanders alone in the wilderness.

GUARD:   Religious, are you? So am I.

*He starts to sing 'Oh Jesus I Have Promised . . .'.*

Night, night, then. Sleep well. There's the 5.45 in the
morning, so if you're up bright and early, you can catch
that.

*More singing, which fades slowly out.*

LILY:   We've got shelter, Colin, and we've got each other.

COLIN:   We've still got tomorrow and tomorrow night and the
next day and the next.

LILY:   We'll manage.

COLIN:   I'm still of the opinion that you should leave me.

LILY:   I won't.

COLIN:   I didn't think you would.

LILY:   Are you glad?

COLIN:   I think so. I think I'm very glad.

*Fade out.*

*Police radio, inside car. Conversation on radio.*

RADIO:   Victoria Wine on High Street – manager lives over the
shop – reported window smashed. Didn't see who did it
but two teenage lads were in the area a few minutes before.
K147, can you investigate?

VOICE:   Okay, Bill. On our way.

RADIO:   Call back if you need any help.

VOICE:   Will do.

RADIO:   And there's a general call to all cars and foot patrols,
keep your eyes open for a couple, man in his late thirties
with a young girl. We've had a call from Preston – they
might have come into our area. Wanted for theft in Preston
and the girl's under age. They're likely to be sleeping rough.

VOICE:   K147 reporting from Victoria Wine.

RADIO:   Go ahead, Phil . . .

*Radio crackles on in background.*

POLICEWOMAN:   Isn't that the couple from the vicarage earlier on?

POLICEMAN:   The broken windows and the fire?

POLICEWOMAN:   The vicar said it was an older man with a young girl. Said he'd told them to go to the bus station.

POLICEMAN:   Let's take a look.

*Car drives off.*

POLICEWOMAN:   *(into radio)*   K152, we've reason to believe the couple from Preston are in the area. Can you give us some details?

RADIO:   Not a lot – the man's Colin Beaumont, aged thirty-eight, the girl's Lily Porter, aged thirteen. She's under a supervision order in Preston. They've been missing two days.

POLICEWOMAN:   We think it's the same two reported at 22.30 by the Vicar of Saint Mary's for broken windows and arson.

RADIO:   Get on to them, then.

POLICEWOMAN:   We're on our way to the bus station. Vicar reports advising them to go there.

RADIO:   If not, try the back of the library or the cinema doorway. You often get dossers spending the night there.

POLICEWOMAN:   Will do.

RADIO:   When you find them, bring them in and we'll get on to Preston.

POLICEWOMAN:   Okay, Bill.   *(To driver)*   They can't have got very far.

POLICEMAN:   We'll find them.

*A heavy-goods train rumbles through again.*

LILY:   *(sleepily)*   A fella came round our way selling insurance. He said that were protection. He told me dad we're allowed five fires a year. We've already had two but they didn't pay much. And me dad's behind wi' t'payments, so I don't suppose we'll get any more.

*Pause.*

You asleep, Colin?

COLIN:   Not really.

LILY:   It's nice here. It's dry and it's not cold. I'm glad he let us stay.

*Pause.*

LILY:   My love . . . come up close and I'll wrap me legs round you.

COLIN:   I'll be heavy on top of you.

LILY:   Try.   *(Pause.)*   Shift your shoulder round a bit. That's it.

COLIN:   I can feel your heart beating very loudly beneath my ear. Bang, bang, bang – your life blood, banging into me.

LILY:   I love the way you talk.

COLIN:   I've always tries to express myself using long words wherever possible. At least I can sound properly educated.

LILY:   It's beautiful talk.

*Pause.*

Comfortable now?

COLIN:   I am. Yes.

You've taught me a lot, you have, Lily, and yet you're only young. I could easily have gone under today if it hadn't been for you. I might have drowned in the emotions occasioned by each different event. It feels like drowning when I get upset. You've taught me to hold my head up, take things as they come. To be honest, you've taught me to rely on God less and myself more – something I'd never have thought possible.

LILY:   It's because I love you, Colin, you know that.

*Pause.*

Where shall we go tomorrow?

COLIN:   *(sleepily)*   I'm all for the Scottish Highlands.

LILY:   By train or thumbing it, this time?

COLIN:   Perhaps we'd better thumb it, travelling by lorry, kings of the road.

LILY:   Knight of the highway.

*Pause.*

COLIN:   I must be getting heavy for you.

LILY:   I like your weight. I like to feel you on me.

*Pause.*

When I were a kiddie, five or six, we had a teacher at school, Miss Grayson. I thought she were beautiful. She smelt nice. I remember her smell, I'd never smelt anyone like that before. The other teachers smelt of parsnips, and in our house, it were all fags and beer and fish and chip papers.

If you got upset or if someone pushed you and you cried, Miss Grayson'd take you on her knee. I used to wish I could cry so I could go on her knee and smell her smell close to. I used to pinch mesel' but it never worked. And once, I pushed a girl who were nasty to me, so she would push me back and make me cry. But they told and she went on Miss Grayson's knee, not me. And I thought to mesel', I'll never go on her knee now, and I never did.

*Pause.*

Daft, eh, the things you remember.

COLIN: One of the worst aspects of prison is the smell.

LILY: Tomorrow, we will go into Boots and spray on some of them testers. They don't like it but they can't get you for it.

*Pause.*

I can see you quite clearly in t'moonlight.

*She sings.*

I see the moon, the moon sees me,
Shining on the leaves of the old oak tree,
Please let the light that shines on me,
Shine on the one I love.

*(Sleepily)* Me nana used to sing that to me – it's a right oldie. Nana smelt of old ladies, but it didn't bother me.

COLIN: Little Lily . . . my love . . .

*They sleep. Fade out.*

*The police car draws up.*

POLICEMAN: What's the time?

POLICEWOMAN: Five-thirty.

POLICEMAN: They'd better bloody well be in there. It's about time we saw some action.

POLICEWOMAN: Come on, then.

*A police siren is heard and a car comes screeching up.*

POLICEMAN:   Now what?

*Car doors slam.*

2nd POLICEMAN:   You've not picked them up yet?

1st POLICEMAN:   We were waiting for you!

2nd POLICEMAN:   Let's go, then.

1st POLICEMAN:   Stay with the car love, eh. And radio in if there's any bother.

POLICEWOMAN:   Thanks, boys.

2nd POLICEMAN:   You go that way, I'll go in the main entrance.

1st POLICEMAN:   Right.

*Footsteps. Brief fade.*

*Inside the waiting-room again.*

LILY:   Colin! I can hear summat. Colin, wake up!

COLIN:   What?

LILY:   I heard a siren.

COLIN:   The police?

LILY:   I don't know. Let's get out of here.

*They get themselves together. Footsteps. The waiting-room door opens. They go out onto the platform.*

1st POLICEMAN:   Eh! Come here!

LILY:   Quick! Across the track.

*They jump down. We hear their feet scrunching over the gravel of the track.*

1st POLICEMAN:   Come here! Come back!

2nd POLICEMAN:   *(into radio)*   Get on to the station, love. We need reinforcements.

*The radio crackles back briefly. A train is heard approaching. Whistle blows. The noise of the train blots everything out for a minute. It fades into panting breath and running footsteps, as* LILY *and* COLIN *run down into the subway.*

COLIN: *(panting)* They'll come looking. They're bound to. It's all up with us.

LILY: Shhh!

1st POLICEMAN: *(shouts)* Where did they get to? Did you see?

2nd POLICEMAN: Bloody train! I didn't see them go out. Try down the subway.

COLIN: Oh God . . .

LILY: Smash t'lights.

*We hear the sound of glass being smashed.*

1st POLICEMAN: *(shouts)* Dave! They're down here! Colin! Lily! Come back. We're going to get you!

LILY: Run, Colin!

*Running footsteps. The policeman also runs.* LILY *and* COLIN *run up the steps the other side of the subway.*

COLIN: We'll never make it.

LILY: Just run.

*Panting breath. Another siren is heard and a car comes screeching up.*

COLIN: Oh God, oh God!

*Car doors slam.*

3rd POLICEMAN: Got you!

*Scuffling noises – shouts.*

Get on after the girl!

COLIN: Run, Lily! Run for freedom!

1st POLICEMAN: Hold out your wrists. Come on. She hasn't got a hope. Thought you could get away, did you?

COLIN: Go on, Lily!

3rd POLICEMAN: Had fun with her, did you, Colin? Fancy them young, eh? They'll want to ask you a few questions about that at the station. Ah! Got her. She can run, can't she? What's the matter with you? Shagged out? Come on, get in the car.

*Car door opens and shuts. Heavy panting breath as LILY is brought up.*

2nd POLICEMAN: Nothing like a good run first thing in the morning. Tones the system up.

POLICEWOMAN: What did you think you were doing, Lily, running away like that?

*Siren. Another police car comes up.*

4th POLICEMAN: Need any help?

1st POLICEMAN: It's okay.

4th POLICEMAN: Right. See you.

*The car drives off again. A car door slams. The car COLIN is in starts up.*

1st POLICEMAN: I'll get lover boy here back to the station.

POLICEWOMAN: She'll have to be got to Preston, somehow or other.

1st POLICEMAN: That's their problem.

LILY: I'm not going to Preston. I'm going wi' Colin.

2nd POLICEMAN: You won't want to go where he's going. Colin's got a lot of talking to do.

LILY:   *(screams)*   Colin!

POLICEWOMAN:   Eh! Come off it! You don't want a slap, do you?

COLIN's *car drives off.*

LILY:   Colin! Can't you see him in there? Can't you see he were crying?

POLICEWOMAN:   In the car. Come on.

*Car door slams.*

See you, lads!

*The other door slams.* LILY's *car drives off.*

*(Inside the car)*   What's in your carrier, Lily? Dear, oh dear, you didn't bring much, did you! What were you going to do about washing and changing your clothes? Nothing very much, by the look of you. The sooner you get a hot bath and wash your hair, the better.

*Pause. The car drives on.*

They'll be sending a car over from Preston for you. Your social worker will probably meet you at the police station and take you to a nice home. That's good, isn't it? They'll be kids your own age there, and you can go to school and forget all this.

*Pause.*

I think you'll be glad to get back, won't you, really and truly? It's all very well, this going off, but it's got you into a lot of trouble – stealing, breaking windows, setting things on fire, that's no way to behave. And what're doing with someone his age, anyway? That's just not right. Once you've settled down, you ought to be very happy in the home. Later on, who knows, they might take you on a youth training scheme where you could do very well – if you try hard. You could put all this behind you.

LILY: Why do you make me leave him? We're happy together. Don't you want us to be happy? Oh Colin, oh Colin!

POLICEWOMAN: You can have a nice cup of tea and then off in another car to Preston.

LILY: You're happy being a policewoman. Why don't you let us be happy? Why? All we want is to be together.

POLICEWOMAN: You know that's not allowed. You should put that right out of your head.

*There is a pause as the car drives along.*

LILY: Colin . . . I'll think of the lovely way you talk and all the things you told me about. I'll think of the caravan we're going to have and the souvenirs we'll collect and I'll love you day and night, whatever they do, or whatever they say. Colin . . . my love, Colin . . .

*The car drives on.*

# MOHICANS
# A LAMENT

*Garry Lyons*

Applications for performance of this play (amateur or
professional) should be directed to Michael Imison Playwrights,
28 Almeida Street, London N1 1TD.

## Cast

SINGER

CUBBY FOX

SNIFFER FOX

CORRIE FOX

*GIRL

*WOMAN WITH THE CROOKED NOSE

VOICE

*Girl and Woman with the Crooked Nose may be played by the Singer.

Where are the blossoms of these summers? — fallen, one by one? so all of my family departed, each in his turn, to the land of the spirits. I am on the hill-top, and must go down into the valley, and when Uncas follows in my footsteps, there will no longer be any of the blood of the sagamores, for my boy is the last of the Mohicans.

James Fenimore Cooper

Setting: The impression of an American Indian campfire. A backdrop of stretched hides in frames. A floor strewn with branches and leaves.

# Scene One

SINGER:

> From Skipton take the A650
> Eastward from the rugged Pennines
> Eastward from the Dales of Yorkshire
> From the limestone cliffs and caverns

CUBBY:

> Down the road where fleece once travelled
> From the sheep's back to the factories
> Down through Keighley, Bingley, Bradford
> Mill towns where the looms once clattered

CORRIE:

> To a dark satanic city
> Sitting on a dark canal bank
> Hard against a dirty river
> Called the Aire despite the smoke-smog

SINGER:

> Leeds! A place of civic splendour
> Proud if ever caked in coke-soot

SNIFFER:

> Theer's nowt wrong wi' 'onest grit, lad
> Ne'er did nobbot 'arm but killed 'em

CUBBY:

> Still, you'll find there ancient tribesmen
> Still at home in ancient homeland
> Back-to-back and pub and terrace
> Washing waving over cobbles

CORRIE:
>    Times, though, are not what they were once
>    For this brave and noble people
>    Homeland due for demolition
>    Poverty, the Great Recession

SNIFFER:
>    Gone the work that was their lifeblood
>    Gone the trades and skills and wages
>    Now the noble tribe of Airedale
>    Lives on what the Social graces

SINGER:
>    Yet this bleak and doleful prospect
>    Can't obliterate a nation –
>    From the depths of deep recession
>    Rises up the young Mohican

# SCENE TWO

*Lights up.* CUBBY *and* SNIFFER *downstage. Leathers, denims, Mohican haircuts. 'Prolecult' fashion of wild West Yorkshire.*

BOTH:    How!

CUBBY:    Easy. First they chomp it off wi' clippers, back from temple. . .

SNIFFER:    So's it's like big letter L behind lug'ole. . .

CUBBY:    Then they grab 'old o' top part an' chop it abaht wi' scissors. . .

SNIFFER:    Yer can use clippers for that an' all, but scissors is more subtle like. . .

CUBBY:    Then they plaster it all wi' Mohican colours. . .

SNIFFER:    Tasteful, yer know – pink or green or owt. . .

CUBBY:  An' then they whack on hair mist, or for really great spike, water an' sugar. . .

SNIFFER:  Fourteen lumps, please . . . real treacle. . .

CUBBY:  Course, if you're right up to date you' 'ave a Davy Crockett – yer know, stripy racoon's tail out back o' bonce. . .

SNIFFER:  An' on bald bit yer can write 'fascist' wi' felt-tip to 'ide your acne. . .

CUBBY:  Then yer walk down t'Headrow, an' it feels . . . well . . . yer know . . . real like. . .

SNIFFER:  Ah! It feels friggin' magic!

CUBBY *glances at him, disapproving.*

# SCENE THREE

CUBBY:  Daily ritual. In t'mornin' the Mohican gets up abaht one o'clock in t'afternoon. . .

SNIFFER:  'Cept on Thursdays when 'e 'as to sign on. . .

CUBBY:  An' scrapes out day before's can o' hairspray. . .

SNIFFER:  An' all bits o' flakey white stuff fall on cassette recorder. . .

CUBBY:  This takes between two an' five minutes dependin' on pain threshold. . .

SNIFFER:  'Cos combin' yer hairspray plays havoc wi' yer scalp-locks. . .

CUBBY:  Then 'e sticks a load o' settin' gel on, or mousse. . .

SNIFFER:  An' 'e gets a piece of hair an' pulls it up as hard as he can. . .

CUBBY:  Then 'e dries it wi' his mother's dryer so's it stands up all stiff an' straight. . .

SNIFFER:   Which is why the Mohican is known by 'is enemy as prickhead. . .

CUBBY:   An' when all t'hair is standin' up like privates on parade, 'e gets a jumbo-size can o' spray an' sprays all t'roots. . .

SNIFFER:   The Mohican allus remembers 'is roots. . .

CUBBY:   Then 'e pulls the hair up at roots an' aims hot blast at 'em wi' dryer. . .

SNIFFER:   So it sets rock solid. . .

CUBBY:   Reinforced concrete. . .

SNIFFER:   Spray's no good for spikes, mind. You need superglue for that. . .

CUBBY:   If the Mohican then thinks it still needs a bit more support 'e sprays over sides an' roots again. Then another quick spray all over an' a bit o' gel on shaved part – an' done! Ready for owt.

SNIFFER:   Superglue's areet but it makes it a bit permanent like. Y' ave to sleep wi' yer chin on piller, like that. *(Demonstrates.)*   Unless yer got a bed wi' special 'ole in. . .

CUBBY:   This ritual takes the Mohican an hour every day. An' 'e gets through three jumbo cans o' hairspray a week. . .

SNIFFER:   D'yer hear abaht the lad who got t'sack 'cos 'e 'ad superglue spikes? Oh, aye. They said 'e were an offence against 'ealth an' safety 'cos 'e were inflammable.

CUBBY:   They said 'e'd be cremated like if 'e came into contact wi' naked flame. That were rubbish really. He were only workin' in t'office.

SNIFFER:   He 'ad last laugh, mind. Wi' all publicity 'e got 'e gorra job down London, modellin' on telly – adverts for 'ealth an' safety at work.

CUBBY: A monthly ritual is washin' the lot. . .

SNIFFER: True, Mohican'd never wash 'is scalp more than that. . .

CUBBY: The gungier it gets, yer see, the better it sticks up. . .

SNIFFER: Sometimes it gets so gungy, yer get little white flakey bits. But when this 'appens yer just stick your nut under tap an' flush 'em out. That way your hair stays good an' slimy.

CUBBY: Function o' scalp-lock dates back, ooh, centuries. . .

SNIFFER: It's so's Mohican stands out in a crowded dole office. . .

CUBBY: An 'aircut in one 'undred. . .

SNIFFER: Style gets yer noticed, right? Like Ultrabrite toothpaste. . .

CORRIE: An' I can't even afford a simple cut an' blow dry.

SNIFFER: The Mohican mother. . .

CUBBY: Generally referred to by the Mohican as 'mam'.


## SCENE FOUR

CORRIE *is carrying a bulging plastic bag.* SNIFFER *flicks the television screen into life. A pulp western is showing.* CUBBY *titivates his barnet.*

CORRIE: What yer watchin' now? It's only two-thirty.

SNIFFER: Telly.

CORRIE: Know what I mean.

SNIFFER: Same as usual. People shootin' each other an' 'avin' mucky dealings wi' crumpet. Dead like life, it is.

CORRIE:   But we agreed, love, dint we? We can't afford to keep it on all t' time. Even if we 'ave nowt else to do.

CUBBY:   Tried to gerrim to purrit off. Yer know what 'e's like.

SNIFFER:   Yah, creep!

CUBBY:   Well, I dunno why yer wanna watch crap.

SNIFFER:   Rather watch it than be full of it.

CUBBY:   What's that s'posed to. . .

CORRIE:   Lads, lads! Yer give me a headache.

CUBBY *produces an official-looking envelope.*

CUBBY:   *(to* CORRIE*)*   This come, second post.

CORRIE:   What is it?

CUBBY *brings it to her.*

CUBBY:   Bright red. Five days or else.

CORRIE: *(taking envelope)*   Oh, no. Electric demand?

CUBBY:   Don't worry, mam. They won't cut us off.

CORRIE:   They threatened to last time.

CUBBY:   They're allus threatenin'.

CORRIE:   Last time they promised.

CUBBY:   Yeah, well, yer know what Government's like at keepin' promises.

SNIFFER:   Where yer been, mam? We want uz snap.

CORRIE:   *(reading demand)*   What? Oh, jumble. Church hall.

CUBBY:   Get owt?

CORRIE:   Mmmn?   *(Looking up)*   Oh, just a coat.

CUBBY:   Let's see, then.

*Picks up the bag, takes it to her.*

CORRIE:   It's nowt.

CUBBY:   Come on.

CORRIE *hesitates, then takes out of the bag a shabby nylon coat which she holds against herself.* CUBBY *does his best to hide disdain.*

CORRIE:   Tried to get summat for you two, but there were nowt worth havin'.

CUBBY:   Just as well.

CORRIE:   Eh?

CUBBY:   I mean, 's alright, mam. I'm kitted out just now.

*She looks at him. Throws down the coat. Slumps into a seat.*

CUBBY:   *(playing with his hair)*   Yeah, well. . .

CORRIE:   How am I gonna pay this bill? T'int as if your dad's paid maintenance for a fortnight. What a day! You'll never guess what 'appened at jumble.

CUBBY:   What?

CORRIE:   Were tryin' coat on in ladies, yer know.

*She puts on the coat, inspecting it for style, size, signs of wear. She puts her hands in the pockets. From one, she pulls out a five-pound note. She looks at it in confusion for a second or two, looks around anxiously, stuffs it back into the pocket, takes off the coat, crosses to a counter.*

'Scuse me. 'Scuse me.

*The* SINGER *turns. She is masked as the* WOMAN WITH THE CROOKED NOSE.

CROOKED NOSE:   Yes? Can I do owt for yer, love?

CORRIE:   This coat.

CROOKED NOSE:   Summat the matter?

CORRIE:   I just wondered – whose is it?

CROOKED NOSE:   Well, yours, love. Yer just bought it, dint yer?

CORRIE:   No, I mean. . . Well, I were just tryin' it on. Put me 'and in pocket. Five-pound note.

*She produces the note.*

CROOKED NOSE:   Well! That's a stroke o' luck.

CORRIE:   But the person must've left it in there.

CROOKED NOSE:   Know what they say – finders keepers.

CORRIE:   Aye, but five pounds! I can't keep that.

CROOKED NOSE:   Go on. It's only paper. Grows on trees.

CORRIE:   I dunno. Dunt seem right.

CROOKED NOSE:   Look, love, if it'll ease your mind – I know woman who gave that coat. She put brass in there on purpose.

CORRIE:   She dint!

CROOKED NOSE:   So purrit away an' spend it on summat nice. An' 'ere, look. There's another to match.

*She brings out another five-pound note.*

CORRIE:   Wha. . .?

CROOKED NOSE:   You deserve it. There's not many'd be as honest as you.

*Places the note in* CORRIE'*s hand and cups the fingers round it.*

CUBBY:   Dunt believe it.

CORRIE:   It's true. I wouldn't lie to yer.

SNIFFER:   No. You ant got imagination.

CORRIE: I dint know whether to take it, or what.

CUBBY: Yer did though?

CORRIE: She insisted. I 'ad no choice.

SNIFFER: Yah, I reckon she nicked it, me.

CORRIE: Wunt while I were outside, I realised who she were.

CUBBY: Who?

CORRIE: Funny ol' woman that runs corner shop.

SNIFFER: Yeah, everyone pinches stuff off 'er.

CUBBY: Ten quid! That's real! Treat yersen. Go on. Go an' gerra perm.

CORRIE: No, I couldn't, love.

CUBBY: Why not? Go on. Yer deserve it.

CORRIE: What abaht electric bill?

SNIFFER: Yeah. An' I got some rabbit at Morrison's earlier. One pound thirty.

CORRIE: All that on meat?

SNIFFER: Yeah. Tell yer what, though – I'll let yer 'ave it for 70p.

CORRIE: Oh no, love. You ant been thievin' again?

SNIFFER: No, it's alright. I dint get caught. Anyway, it's all for a good cause.

CORRIE: What cause?

SNIFFER: Best one o' lot. Uz guts.

CUBBY: Oh, aye. Charity begins at 'ome.

CORRIE: You two'll be the death o' me. I know we're hard up. But that int the way, love. I dint bring you up all these years to be little criminals.

SNIFFER:   Who were it then? Must've been someone.

CORRIE:   Oh, do your own dinner!

*Storms out.*

CUBBY:   What d'yer talk to 'er like that for? Eh? Christ! Wouldn't mind, 'cept I get lumped in.

SNIFFER:   Can't stand it. All 'er whingin' an' whinin' on.

CUBBY:   Leave 'er alone. She 'as 'er bit o' fun. Her Valium an' 'er *Sun* crossword

SNIFFER:   'S what she deserves. It's the only way to get her to do owt for uz. Bullyin'.

CUBBY:   Rubbish. Yer should try bein' more subtle with 'er. Mothers are like that. You 'ave to know 'em. Work 'em round gradually. They're like fruit machines. You play 'em all t' while but they only pay out every so often.

SNIFFER:   Oh, listen to 'im!

CUBBY:   Well, yer should study my technique, kid.

*To them,* CORRIE.

CORRIE:   Cubby!

CUBBY:   Ey up.   *(To* CORRIE*)*   Yeah, mam. What d'yer want?

CORRIE:   Have I 'ad your keep this week, love?

CUBBY:   Oh, no. Sorry. Meant to say. Had a few expenses like. That job interview, Tuesday.

CORRIE:   Expenses?

CUBBY:   Well, yer know. Had to do summat wi' me hair.

CORRIE:   Oh, love. An' I can't afford decent dandruff shampoo. Well, you'll just 'ave to gi' me all your next week's Giro, won't yer?

CUBBY:   I will?

CORRIE:  Aye.

SNIFFER:  Jackpot, Cubs! Bloody jackpot!

# SCENE FIVE

*Tom-toms.* CORRIE *puts on her coat.*

SINGER:

Pity the Mohican mother
Bringing up Mohican brothers
Fatherless Mohican brothers
On the dole and on the breadline
Owing dough 'til final deadline
Living hard against the deadline
Ruthless, brutal, final deadline –
Scrounger! cries the banner headline!

CORRIE:  Hello . . . 'scuse me . . . I said, 'scuse me . . . I've
come abaht me electric bill . . . well, final demand . . .
yeah, that's right . . . now it says 'ere  *(Waving
demand)*  if you are 'avin' difficulty in payin' this
account, you are urged to contact us at the above as quickly
. . . What?. . . Well, I only gorrit yesterday . . . Oh . . .
right. It's Fox . . . Mrs Corrie . . . well, Cora, really . . .
Cora . . . no, one 'r' . . . Alice Fox . . . yes . . . 13
Hudson Terrace . . . Woodhouse . . . Leeds 6 . . . yes,
I'm claimin' supplementary . . . what? . . . Oh . . . next
floor up . . .

SINGER:

Next floor up and lift not working
Corridors with faces smirking
Made to feel she's only shirking
Pity the Mohican mother!

CORRIE:  Hello . . . I've come abaht this . . . Fox . . . Mrs Cora
. . . no, one 'r' . . . Alice Fox . . . 13 . . . no, thirteen . . . Hudson Terrace . . . Woodhouse . . . Leeds 6
. . .

No, it's still standin' . . . they ant knocked it down yet
. . . aye, supplementary, yeah . . . What? . . . Oh, but
they told me downstairs it were 'ere I should go . . . Next
one up . . .

SINGER:
Separate floors for poor and wealthy
Separate laws for sick and healthy
Life's a trial and she's made guilty
Pity the Mohican mother!

CORRIE:   Hello . . . is this where yer deal wi' folk on
supplementary? . . . At last . . . been all over . . . It's me
final demand . . . Well . . . yer see . . . it's like this . . .
Things are a bit 'ard up at the moment, like . . . Fox . . .
Mrs Cora . . . Oh, look, there it is. . .

*She points to her address on the bottom of the demand.*

. . . 13 . . . yes . . . unlucky for some, yes . . .
Supplementary . . . two sons . . . both on supplementary,
too . . . Eh? . . . yer mean I can't see nobody now? . . .
Well when, then? . . . tomorrer . . . well, I don't know
. . . Look, I've come all this way . . . are yer sure I can't
see no-one today? . . . Mister . . . listen . . . did yer 'ear
what I said? . . . Eh, mister, I said: did yer 'ear what I said?
. . .

SINGER:   And that's why they call them faceless bureaucrats.

## Scene Six

CUBBY *and* SNIFFER *sit at a table. Condiments, sauce bottles,
plastic tomato.*

CUBBY:   Mohican diet. Dole day dinner's down t'Buffalo Burger
Bar.

SNIFFER:   Original American twice! An' four lots o' Frenchies
wi' scraps on, ta pal!

CUBBY: This meal is known to Mohican as . . .

SNIFFER: Magic trough.

*He opens up a tabloid.*

CUBBY: Religion. Some Mohicans worship the *Sun*.

SNIFFER: Phwah-ee! Look at Tina!

CUBBY: But this is by no means a universal conviction. *(To*
SNIFFER*)* Keep it to yersen.

SNIFFER: *(turning to back)* Fancy a flutter on three-thirty?

CUBBY: Huh. Know what they say, don't yer?

SNIFFER: What?

CUBBY: Only thing worth purrin' on a horse is Lady Godiva.

SNIFFER: *(turning back to page three)* An' there she is!

CUBBY: *(pushing paper away)* Yer know, that rag's gorra
readin' age of eight an' a half. Kid of eight could read that.
It's the opium o' people.

SNIFFER: What's opium, then?

CUBBY: Eh?

SNIFFER: What's opium mean?
*Pause*

CUBBY: Yeah, well. Proves me point.

SNIFFER: Ah! Yer don't even know, yersen.

CUBBY: Aye, I do. It's a kind o' drug.

SNIFFER: Yer need drugs these days. Time-killers. So's time
don't kill you. Read it in 'ere other day. Things are gerrin'
so bad in some parts o' country ' wi' dole an' frustration
an' that – that even them Good Samaritans are toppin'
theirsens. Aye. Yer ring 'em up an' yer get one o' them
answerphones.

CUBBY:   Int funny, yer know. Reckon mam'll be takin' an overdose if things go on.

SNIFFER:   Talkin' o' drugs.

*Surreptitiously opens his jacket and pulls out a can of glue.*

CUBBY:   Where d'yer get that?

SNIFFER:   GCSE top grade shoplifter, me.

CUBBY:   Wazzock! You'll get nicked.

SNIFFER:   You do it.

CUBBY:   Aye, things I need.

SNIFFER:   Oh, aye. Tell that to judge.

CUBBY:   That stuff's illegal in Scotland, yer know.

SNIFFER:   So what do they do when heel comes off their boot? Stick it back on again wi' porridge?

CUBBY:   They can allus trump up summat. Breach o' peace or owt. 'Sides, it destroys your brain. Makes yer forget stuff.

SNIFFER:   You used to sniff.

CUBBY:   When?

SNIFFER:   Don't say yer don't remember.

CUBBY:   I don't.

SNIFFER:   You're right. It does destroy brain. Couple o' year back. Used to come 'ome wi' it all down your front.

CUBBY:   Once maybe. Twice at most.

SNIFFER:   An' the rest.

CUBBY:   Alright. Enough to know what a bad one's like.

SNIFFER: I've 'ad a bad one too, yer know. It were so bad I thought I were out o' work since leaving school wi' no chance o' gerrin' a job. Think o' that.

CUBBY: An' don't wave it abaht in 'ere, neither!

*Snatches can away.* SNIFFER *looks at him contemptuously.*

SNIFFER: Allus another where that'n came from.

*Takes out food bag, plays with it.*

CUBBY: Look, yer can sniff yersen into grave, far as I'm concerned. It's mam I'm worried abaht. What's she gonna do when yer come 'ome reekin', or yer suffocate your bloody sen in bag?

SNIFFER: Well, you int such a superstar, yersen.

CUBBY: Least I'm thinkin'. Least I'm tryin' to use me time.

SNIFFER *picks up plastic tomato. Starts squeezing sauce from the plastic tomato into the food bag.*

What yer doin' now? Sniffin' sauce?

SNIFFER: We're short o' ketchup at 'ome.

CUBBY: Gizzit 'ere!

*Snatches the bag away.*

Christ! You're a liability, you.

SNIFFER: Oh? Is that good or bad?

CUBBY: Can't yer take owt seriously?

SNIFFER: Aye. When it int funny like.

CUBBY: Dah! Wash me 'ands o' yer. I int 'angin' round 'ere waitin' for trouble. You're nowt but a dosser – a little sniffglue.

*Makes away.*

SNIFFER:   Where yer goin'?

CUBBY:   Dunno.

SNIFFER:   What abaht your burger?

CUBBY:   Eat it yersen.

   *Goes.*

SNIFFER:   Magic. Four lots o' chips. Ace!

   *Buries his head in the* Sun.

   Little Sniffglue. Mmmmn. That's a name that could stick.

# SCENE SEVEN

*During the following speech,* SNIFFER *takes out the food bag, buries his face in it, and breathes. The bag expands and contracts like an artificial lung.*

CUBBY:   The Mohican allus uses t'make that smells strongest. Well, there are others that smell stronger but they're so strong yer can't take 'em. So 'e gets 'is Evostick an' 'e goes up Woodhouse Ridge. It's a good place for a session 'cos there's loads o' trees like. An' 'e starts sniffin'. An' all round e' sees all these illusions. Great big space invaders on wall. An' spirits jumpin' out at 'im from behind woods. Nice spirits . . . well, yer know, at first. But then trees start to move. An' eyes start to follow 'im. Policeman's eyes or 'is mam's eyes or summat. An' 'e begins to run. But they keep on followin'. An' 'e can't get away. An' they're still comin' after 'im. An' 'is feet leave ground. He's goin' up an' up. Up an' up towards clouds. An' next thing 'e knows, 'e's wakin' up on ground in a puddle o' sick. An' 'e starts thinkin': there's some kids around Leeds that've been at it for years – sniffin'. An' they can't even talk straight 'cos their brains are sort o' rotted away. An' when 'e thinks o' that 'e starts to think: it int worth it, is it? I mean, yer know, it can't be worth it.

# Scene Eight

*Tom-toms.*

CORRIE:  Fox . . . aye . . . aye . . . Leeds 6 . . . aye . . . What?
. . . council wunt confirm 'ow much rent I'm paying . . .
Why not! I see . . . well . . . I better go there, then . . .

# Scene Nine

CUBBY:  War. Traditionally the Mohican went on warpath every
Saturday . . .

SNIFFER:  Elland Road or away venue . . .

CUBBY:  He'd prepare 'imsen by puttin' on traditional warrior's
get-up . . .

SNIFFER:  Bovver jacket . . . Doc Martens . . .

CUBBY:  Pumps if 'e's plannin' on makin' a runner . . .

SNIFFER:  White scarf round 'is neck . . . sometimes trimmed
wi' blue an' yeller . . .

CUBBY:  Rattle . . . flick knife . . . an' broken bottle . . .

SNIFFER:  Mohican allus 'as plenty o' bottle . . .

CUBBY:  Then the 'ole tribe'd collect at Vicar Lane bus
station . . .

SNIFFER:  By 52 stop, behind kiosk . . .

CUBBY:  An' summon divine aid from their gods an' 'eroes wi'
mythical chants an' incantations . . .

BOTH:  One Norman Hunter
There's only one Norman Hunter
One Billy Bremner
There's only one Donald Revie!

CUBBY:  Then they'd all gerron bus an' go down Lower
Wortley . . .

SNIFFER:   An' wait outside ground to ambush opposition.

*They wait, stealthily, then suddenly leap into a vigorous fight mime.*

CUBBY:   An' they'd just be gerrin' stuck in when it'd be . . .

SNIFFER:   *(siren noise)*   Na-na, na-na, na-na, na-na!

CUBBY:   So they'd beat the 'ell out of it . . .

SNIFFER:   Jump over turnstiles wi' out payin' . . .

CUBBY:   An' launch assault on enemy terraces . . .
*(Whoops and cries. More fight mime.)*

SNIFFER:   Or sometimes, they'd just taunt 'em an' tease 'em . . .
war chants to get t'other side really riled . . .

BOTH:   You're goin' 'ome in a Yorkshire ambulance!

*(Clap to the rhythm.)*

You're goin' home in a Yorkshire ambulance!

CUBBY:   But all them 'alcyon days are past . . .

SNIFFER:   Days when Mohican swept all before 'im . . .
followin' 'is side on conquests o' Europe . . .

CUBBY:   Leeds United were relegated to Second Division . . .
an' the brave an' noble Mohican suffered t'ignominy o'
skirmishin' wi' likes o' Grimsby . . .

SNIFFER:   Barnsley . . .

CUBBY:   An' Huddersfield Town.

SNIFFER:   Then blue cavalry in metal chargers broke up these
ceremonial scraps . . .

CUBBY:   Wi' wristlocks an' 'ittin' sticks an' crying smoke that
makes yer blind . . .

SNIFFER:   An' they started vettin' ticket sales . . .

CUBBY:   There were no more o' this straddlin' turngates . . .

SNIFFER:   So noble savage 'ad nowt to do . . . just sit at 'ome wi' tobacco an' firewater . . .

CUBBY:   An' watch wrestlin' on telly . . .

*Wrestling on the television. The Mohicans sit and watch with blank expressions for a good while.*

It int no substitute for doin' it yersen.

## SCENE TEN

*Tom-toms.*

CORRIE:   Mrs Cora Alice . . . Wha? . . . What? . . . Sort it out wi' 'ousin' benefits? . . . But it's Saturday . . . Saturday . . . Well, I mean . . . they're closed . . .

## SCENE ELEVEN

CUBBY *titivating his hair.*

CUBBY:   Saturday night. Chingachgook's. Disco, yer know. Centre o' Leeds. Yer spruce up your plumage. Purron best bleach denims. An' off out. Bird 'untin'. Well, yer don't call it that no more 'cos it's sexist. But yer can't argue wi' nature, can yer? So yer get to club, right? Bloke comes up. Dickie bow an' jacket job.

SNIFFER *in black jacket.*

SNIFFER:   *(as bouncer)*   All right, Geronimo, where you off to?

CUBBY:   Goin' in.

SNIFFER:   Sorry, pal. No Red Indians. Cowboy night tonight.

CUBBY:   Don't mess us abaht. Just let us in, eh?

SNIFFER:   I said. This is a civilised place. Never let Mohicans in. It's a rule.

CUBBY:   Since when?

SNIFFER:   Since they were wiped out abaht eighteen 'undred an' summat. What's it feel like to be part of an extinct tribe?

CUBBY:   I've been in 'undreds o' times.

SNIFFER:   Scoutin' for squaws is it?   *(Shows a rampant forearm)*   Battle o' the Little Big Horn.   *(Forearm limp)*   Or maybe Custer's Last Stand, eh?

CUBBY:   I'm just 'ere to enjoy mesen.

SNIFFER:   Well, I can't let yer in, pal. Not lookin' like that.

CUBBY:   Why not?

SNIFFER:   Well, look at yer, eh?   *(Pause.)*   You int gorra tie on.

*CUBBY glares at him, takes off his belt, wraps it with a bow round his neck.*

CUBBY:   Suit yer?

SNIFFER:   *(smirking)*   Smart.

CUBBY:   Dunno why *you're* laughin', pal. Not in that gerrup. Don't even fit yer. That jacket 'angs off yer like a curtain. Folk 'ave to peep through it to see if you're in. Now, now. Don't turn nasty. 'S all style, in' it? Haircuts, dinner jacket. 'Sall makin' statement. Difference is, I'm being different. My statement's me own. You're just sayin' summat somebody's told yer to.

SNIFFER:   An' gerrin' paid for it.

CUBBY:   Ah, yer see. You're just selling out. I'm the only one that's expressin' 'imsen 'ere. But, if yer don't mind, I'd rather go an' express mesen in there, an' let yer get on wi' your job.

*Walks past him.*

# Scene Twelve

*Loud disco music. Flashing lights.*

CUBBY:   In time past, the Mohican evolved an elaborate code o' greetin'. On enterin' a smoky disco or night club 'e would approach 'is brother, slap 'im across shoulder, an' say: Watchyer tosspot, mine's a Tetley's. To which the reply would generally be . . .

SNIFFER:   Jump in t'lake, pal. Yer 'ad one off me last week.

CUBBY:   If it were, the Mohican would know that 'is brother were on friendly terms. An' conversation would continue in this manner while one or t'other were persuaded into buyin' a round. The recent rapid decline in Mohican fortunes, 'owever, 'as made its mark on such customs. Openin' formality is now more likely to be: We stoppin' for a sup, then? To which retort might be . . .

SNIFFER:   'Ow much yer got?

CUBBY:   I can only buy one for mesen.

SNIFFER:   Me too. At a pinch like.

CUBBY:   We could 'ave *one* then?

SNIFFER:   'Ave to skip picture, mind.

CUBBY:   Bevvy's cheaper. Make it last all evenin'.

SNIFFER:   Right.

*They drink.*

CUBBY:   Disco! The initiation, where Mohican manhood's first unsheathed . . .

SNIFFER:   As soon as a Mohican male passes age o' puberty 'e is obliged by 'is forefathers to find a partner . . .

CUBBY: In Mohican society, members of opposite gender act out a strictly ordered series o'courtship games as preamble to matrimony or sexual intercourse . . .

SNIFFER: These int necessarily same thing . . .

CUBBY: Initial attraction occurs when both parties send out code signs in culturally acquired body language . . .

*He is sitting. To him, the* SINGER, *as the* GIRL. *He is eyeing her up. She notices, acts demur. He plays cool, stands up, takes out a cigarette, lights it, fumbles with it, recovers. She looks round, he catches her eye, they smile at each other, he moves in for the kill, offering the cigarette with a passable teenage attempt at machismo confidence. She pushes it aside. Walks away.*

GIRL: No, ta.

CUBBY: The code is complex an' open to misinterpretation, but it's also flexible enough to express a whole range of emotions . . .

*Dances.* GIRL *returns. They catch each other's eye, turn away shyly.*

GIRL: Hi, Cubby.

CUBBY: Hi.

GIRL: What's up?

CUBBY: Oh, things.

*Pause.*

GIRL: What?

CUBBY: It's 'ome. Course.

GIRL: What abaht it?

CUBBY: Oh. Mam can't pay lecky bill while 'ousin' benefits pay uz rent, so we'll be cut off. And dad wunt pay 'is maintenance. An' our kid's started sniffin' glue. An' I'm glad yer come, yer know. Thought yer wunt gonna.

*Pause.*

GIRL: Try an' stop me.

CUBBY: Really?

*Pause.*

Course.

CUBBY *makes a clumsy grab for her hand.*

CUBBY: Look, why don't we go away? Leave all this. Just us two.

GIRL: What d'yer mean?

CUBBY: Go. Anywhere. It dunt matter. London, Australia, owt. America. Yeah, that's it. New York. Anywhere wi' a bit of 'ope on offer. What d'yer say? I could gerra job. We both could. An' if it worked out like, we could . . . I dunno . . . maybe . . . get married . . . start a family like. Well, if yer wanted to.

GIRL: When?

CUBBY: Now. Tomorrer. Tonight. Come on.

GIRL: *(affectionate)* Oh, you're mad.

*Pause.*

CUBBY: You're all right, you.

GIRL: You'll do, yersen. Spite o' your mop.

*Pushes her hand through his scalp-lock. They smile. Embrace. Are about to kiss when* CUBBY *suddenly breaks out of the clinch.*

CUBBY: Course this is a scene from Mohican myth. The reality is more likely to be summat like this . . .

*Sitting.* GIRL *approaches.*

GIRL:   Ey up, misery guts. What yer sulkin' for?

CUBBY:   Nowt that'll worry you.

GIRL:   Oh, yeah? Shift your ass. I'm sittin' down.

> CUBBY *sighs, shifts in his seat. She sits next to him.*

Buyin' me a drink, then?

CUBBY:   Skint.

GIRL:   Oh, like that, is it?

CUBBY:   Truth.

GIRL:   Oh, aye.   *(Pause.)*   Run out o' words to say an' all, is it?   *(Pause.)*   Look, what's gorrin' to yer?

CUBBY:   Nowt.

GIRL:   Must be summat. Not your usual stroppy sen, are yer?

CUBBY:   It's 'ome, if yer must know.

GIRL:   Ah-h, can't your mam pay lecky bill again?

CUBBY:   'Ow d'you know?

GIRL:   Well, it int first time it's 'appened, is it?

CUBBY:   Dunt make it owt easier.

*Pause.*

GIRL:   Oh, look. I'm sorry.

CUBBY:   Yeah.

GIRL:   I am.

CUBBY:   I know.

GIRL:   Dunt sound as if yer do.

CUBBY:   Yer said yer were, dint yer?

GIRL: Yeah . . .

CUBBY: Well then, you're flamin' sorry, aren't yer?

*Pause.*

GIRL: I'm sorry. *(Pause.)* Look, is there owt I can do? I wanna help. Really.

CUBBY: Do yer?

GIRL: Yeah.

CUBBY: *(face brightening)* D'yer fancy a quick one, then?

*Pause.*

GIRL: Tell yer what, I'll get them drinks in.

*She gets up.* CUBBY *grabs her hand.*

CUBBY: Serious offer. Come on. Don't yer fancy it? For a change, like.

GIRL: What, trial run?

CUBBY: Just for a laugh.

GIRL: Here?

CUBBY: Don't be daft. Find somewhere private. There's this snicket by marketplace.

*Pause.*

GIRL: Would an' all, wouldn't yer?

CUBBY: Come on.

*Pause.*

GIRL: No.

CUBBY: What?

GIRL: No.

CUBBY:   Why?

GIRL:   I can't.

CUBBY:   Can't?

GIRL:   It's me . . . yer know . . .

CUBBY:   What?

GIRL:   Me time.

CUBBY:   Your monthlies?

GIRL:   Sssh! Don't have to tell everyone.

CUBBY:   I know yer want to.

GIRL:   I don't. Not at the moment.

*Pause.*

CUBBY:   Huh. Just an excuse, in it? Real reason is yer don't fancy me.

GIRL:   Well, what d'yer expect? You'd understand if you were a girl.

*Pause.*

CUBBY:   Yeah. Okay. *(Pause.)* Christ. *(Pause.)* Tell uz summat, will yer? Don't laugh now. I mean it. What's wrong wi' me? I mean, why can I never seem to get it right wi' lasses? I just dunt seem to 'ave the technique.

GIRL:   Oh, bloody Nora! Don't start that tack.

CUBBY:   What now?

GIRL:   I can't stand sensitive fellers.

CUBBY:   I'm serious.

GIRL:   Look, you're not a bad sort o' bloke, as blokes go, Cubby. But I'm not purrin' it abaht for t'sake of it.

CUBBY:   Oh, do us a favour. It's well too late for you to become a virgin.

GIRL:   What?

CUBBY:   What 'appened to Women's Lib?

GIRL:   Women's Lib? I'm eighteen, I'm unemployed, an' I come from Batley. How am I s'posed to know abaht Women's Lib? I'm sorry!

*She goes.*

CUBBY:   Sod it!

# SCENE THIRTEEN

*Disco music.*

SNIFFER:   Chingachgook's on a Saturday night! The style council of all the subcults . . .

CUBBY:   Skinheads . . .

SNIFFER:   Punks . . .

CUBBY:   New romantics . . .

SNIFFER:   Rockers . . .

CUBBY:   Teds . . .

SNIFFER:   Rastafari . . .

CUBBY:   Bowie freaks an' weird transvestites . . .

SNIFFER:   Boy George clones an' gender benders . . .

CUBBY:   Heavy metal an' 'ippie retreads . . .

SNIFFER:   Radical fems an' trendy lefties . . .

CUBBY:   Culture Club o' modern Britain . . .

SNIFFER:   Human League o' newest England . . .

CUBBY: This confusion o' teenage groupings were a particular feature o' nineteen eighties. The great tie o' musical taste, an' island o' common class origin, were severed in many places. An' it were one o' consequences that skinhead an' rude boy were found street fightin' in the same ranks, while Nazi sought scalp o' Anti-Nazi, though it were believed they came from same stock. An' Mohicans were divided among theirsens. Love for traditional values kept a small band under red banner o' Labour Party but a larger number were known to be supporters o' Apathy League.

SNIFFER: An' tragedy were that teenage once lived in relative peace. All wi' long hair an' stoned on dope. But love an' peace, anyway. An' then came what they called the Big Slump, one o' greatest apocalyptic events o' Mohican legend. Suddenly, overnight, all tribesmen lost their jobs, an' they just tramped streets wi' nowt to do. An' then they started dressin' up – to relieve boredom, reacquire lost identity. An' that's 'ow friend divided from friend, an' natural enemies began to look similar.

CUBBY: 'Cos what 'appened then were the death o' prolecult. All t'middle-class kids in polys an' art schools ripped off the fashions that dole queue 'ad started. An' haircuts an' ear-rings lost subversive meanin', an' just became, like, decoration. This turmoil were t'famous Style Wars o' late seventies an' early eighties. An' at the end, Mohican supremacy were left in tatters. Well, tatters an' zips an' tattoos an' stuff. An' then there emerged a new phenomenon. A wah-wah speakin' paleface, relic o' British Empire. His name, need I tell yer? The Sloane Ranger.

# SCENE FOURTEEN

*William Tell Overture.* SNIFFER *as the Sloane Ranger.*

SNIFFER: *(upper-crust accent)* By God, Tonto, old bean! Fancy meeting you here. What are you up to, old fruit?

CUBBY:  Well . . .

SNIFFER:  No, don't tell me. Having a crack at some skirt, yes? Naughty, Tonto. All the same, you oiks, once you're left off the old lead. Bet you're wondering what I'm doing in this ghastly rathole? Well, rather long story, really. I was up at Ilkley this afters, hunting.

CUBBY:  Deer?

SNIFFER:  No, Tonto. Table mats. Trying to complete my Georgian collection. Dashed bad luck, though. Not a sausage.

CUBBY:  Oh.

SNIFFER:  Someone had snapped 'em up earlier in the week. Some North Country Charlie who works in systems analysis, no doubt. What a waste. Anyway, I'd arranged to meet a few of my old muckers from Ampleforth – sample a few tinctures at the local hostelry. Well, I tell you, the gin and tonics in Ilkley are absolutely kosher. And, to be perfectly frank, we all got a bit tired and emotional, and Nigel went over the hill in a very senior way. There we were, surrounded by all these po-faced Yorkshire Ramsbottoms, with Nigel deliberately falling over backwards off his pine alpino seat. Whump! Well, on the fourth or fifth occasion, the bar staff are getting a little frisky, so we decide to beat a hasty retreat. Jump into my dinky, absolutely paralytic, slap the band of the Blues and Royals on the cassette, and belt up here to see what the native debs can do in the way of party tricks. What's the matter, old man? Something troubling you?

CUBBY *is nervously trying to draw* SNIFFER*'s attention to something.*

CUBBY:  Er . . . there could be some aggro 'ere.

SNIFFER:  Aggro? Is this something to do with your native sixth sense?

CUBBY:   No, it's starin' yer right in face. Look at that skinhead.

SNIFFER:   What, that chap with the kojak?

CUBBY:   Sssh! Chris' sake, don't gerrim wild.

SNIFFER:   What about him? Seems quite house-trained.

CUBBY:   Yer see way 'e's pickin' 'is teeth wi' flick-knife?

SNIFFER:   Yes.

CUBBY:   Well, don't yer know what it means?

SNIFFER:   Oh, you mean it's a primitive kind of communication?

CUBBY:   Aye, if yer like.

SNIFFER:   How fascinating! Well, go on. Translate, man.

CUBBY:   Well, it dunt take much . . . it means a punch-up.

SNIFFER:   Fisticuffs?

CUBBY:   At very least.

SNIFFER:   With yours truly?

CUBBY:   'Fraid so.

SNIFFER:   Well, I say! That's not cricket.

CUBBY:   Maybe. But we'll 'ave to do summat – an' fast.

SNIFFER:   You think so?

CUBBY:   Aye. He's gorra dozen mates. An' they've just surrounded us.

SNIFFER:   That's a bit stiff. It's a democratic country.

CUBBY:   Look, why dunt I 'old 'em at bay wi' me hai-karate, an' you make a break for nearest fire exit?

SNIFFER:   No, no, no Tonto. Wouldn't hear of it. That's not what they taught you to do at Sandhurst.

CUBBY:   Well, we gorra do summat.

SNIFFER:   Don't fret, old fruit. I've a much better tactic. The old man was in the foreign office. He always said: When a chap gets in a spot, his strongest weapon is the art of diplomacy.

CUBBY:   They don't look too diplomatic to me.

SNIFFER:   *(calling out)*   I say! I say, you chaps with the army hair-dos. Very well turned out indeed, I must say. Now then, hope you're going to give my friend and me safe passage to the front door. What's that? *(To CUBBY)* I didn't quite catch it.

CUBBY:   Well, basically 'e said: Go away!

SNIFFER:   *(calling)*   Exactly. That's what we're trying to do. Look, I've got a few crispy pondos here.   *(Put out)*   Oh. Well, if they won't be reasonable.   *(Calling)*   Now come on, you lot. Play the white man. I happen to be related to three high court judges, five QCs and a prominent member of the House of Lords.

CUBBY:   It int workin', Sloane Ranger. Let's run for it.

SNIFFER:   Nonsense. Where will we all be in the future if we yield to bullyboys and thugs?

CUBBY:   Alive. Christ, 'ere they come!

SNIFFER:   Now look, scum. This'll hurt you more than it does me.

CUBBY:   Don't be mad, Sloane Ranger. Quick, let's go!

*He cowers.*

SNIFFER:   I'm warning you. Don't come any closer, now.

CUBBY:   Sloane Ranger! Behind!

*SNIFFER turns swiftly, pulling a revolver from his pocket, and empties several cartridges. Silence. SNIFFER surveys the scene smugly, blows across the barrel of the gun.* CUBBY *slowly rises from his cowering stance.*

CUBBY:   But . . . but yer killed 'em, Sloane Ranger.

SNIFFER:   Yes. That'll teach these working-class hoodlums a moral lesson, Tonto.

CUBBY:   What moral lesson?

SNIFFER:   One that every good schoolboy knows. You don't flaming well mess with the Sloane Ranger. Hi-ho, Silver – away!

*Canters away to the William Tell Overture.*

## SCENE FIFTEEN

*Tom-toms.*

SINGER:

They came with biro pens and clipboards
Armed with stats and urban studies
Paleface men in polyester
Southern men with smiles and handshakes
Pushed us from our ancient homeland
Back-to-back and pub and terrace
When will our time come again?
Oh, when will our time come again?

## SCENE SIXTEEN

SNIFFER *and* CORRIE *are watching television. Pulp western.*

CUBBY:   Mohican Sunday is marred by a weekly ordeal called Access. This is when the Mohican father returns from his labours in t'world abroad to visit his expectant offspring. *(Opening door to an invisible character)*   Oh, hi. You're late.

*Pause.*

Yeah, well, yer might as well come in, I s'pose.

SNIFFER: *(leaping up)* Oh, magic! Yer made it, then?

*Unusually friendly, he rushes over to do some shadow boxing with the invisible character.*

How's it goin', then? Yeah, I'm all right.

CORRIE: Oh, you're 'ere, then?

*Pause.*

Don't apologise to me. It's lads I'm thinkin' of.

SNIFFER: Wanna cup o' tea, mate?

*Pause.*

Why? Where you goin'?

*Pause.*

Oh. I see.

*Pause.*

CORRIE: Why d'yer bother comin' round at all, if yer int gonna stop?

CUBBY: Don't upset yersen, mam. If 'e don't want us to see 'im, 'e don't want us to see 'im.

*Pause.*

What's money situation like this week, love?

*Pause.*

Well, I was wonderin', like. Maintenance.

*Pause.*

I know, love. It's just that . . . well, they're gonna cut electrics off. I can't go on like this.

*Pause.*

Well, you are three week behind, love. What do yer expect me to do?

*Pause.*

CUBBY:   *(to audience)*   An' so it goes on. Just like 'e dunt even exist.

# SCENE SEVENTEEN

*Light change,* SINGER *masks up as the* WOMAN WITH THE CROOKED NOSE, *and goes behind the table.*

CUBBY:   Corner shop is traditional centre o' Mohican community . . . where 'e goes for chat . . . an' stock up wi' provisions. The Mohican goes in t' shop . . generally takes companion with 'im . . . an' clocks which sweet jar's right in corner on top shelf.   *(Whispers to* SNIFFER*)*   Mint 'umbugs!

CROOKED NOSE:   Hello, lads. What can we do for yer?

SNIFFER:   Quarter o' mint 'umbugs, please.

CROOKED NOSE:   *(turns her back to them, looks across shelves )* Mint 'umbugs, mint 'umbugs . . .

SNIFFER:   *(pointing)*   They're up there. Can yer see?

CROOKED NOSE:   Oooh, I'll 'ave to get a chair.

*Gets chair, stands on it, reaches up to shelf.*

SNIFFER:   Left a bit . . . left a bit . . . stop . . . right a bit . . . no, yer got liquorice all-sorts.

CUBBY:   Then while ol' woman's trying to get 'umbugs, all these items start leapin' unexpectedly into Mohican's pockets . . . like they got spirits o' their own or summat . . . *(Produces items in turn)*   One kingsize packet o' Silk Cut . . . Mars bar . . . bag o' salt an' vinegar crisps . . . two packs o' Orbit chewy . . . one jumbo-size can o' hairspray. How the Great Spirit doth provide!

CROOKED NOSE:   No. It's no good, love. D'yer wanna try it?

SNIFFER:   No. 'S alright. I'll 'ave some wine gums.

CROOKED NOSE:   Wine gums. Now I think they're down 'ere.

*Gets off chair, bends down under counter, emerges holding a hunting rifle. She points it at the lads.*

Now, yer can put back all yer pinched.

*Pause.*

CUBBY:   What?

CROOKED NOSE:   Come on. Hawk-eyes, me.

CUBBY *and* SNIFFER *look at each other.* CUBBY *reluctantly gives her the Mars bar, crisps and chewing gum.*

And the rest.

CUBBY:   That's it.

CROOKED NOSE:   *(waving gun)*   Don't be silly.

CUBBY:   All right.
*Hands over cigarettes.*

CROOKED NOSE:   Hairspray.

CUBBY:   Ant got no hairspray.

CROOKED NOSE:   Gorra nasty growth where yer shouldn't 'ave, then.

CUBBY *hands over the hairspray.*

Now, d'yer wanna pay for any o' this?

CUBBY:   Skint.

CROOKED NOSE:   You too?

SNIFFER:   Society's to blame, missus.

CROOKED NOSE:  Well, be on your way, then. Don't try nowt like that again.

*The lads turn to go. The woman stops them.*

If you'd been honest in t'first place, you'd've gorrit for nowt, yer know.

*She holds out the hairspray.*

Go on. Take it.

CUBBY:  For nowt?

CROOKED NOSE:  Aye. Your dad'll kill me, I should think. But it's your 'air, int it?

*Pause.*

SNIFFER:  *(going for the spray)*  We dunt exactly 'ave a dad . . .

CUBBY *pulls him back.*

CUBBY:  No-one 'as to give charity to uz. Uz Foxes dunt take 'andouts.

## Scene Eighteen

CORRIE *walks, head bowed, towards a chair. She is weeping profusely, and holds a kitchen knife in front of her. She slumps down.*

SNIFFER:  That dunt mean yer shouldn't take it.

CUBBY:  I dunt care. No-one owes uz nowt. An' we dunt owe no-one.

SNIFFER:  Wanna bet?

CUBBY *notices* CORRIE.

Ssssh!

SNIFFER:  Numero uno. That's the only one that counts.

CUBBY:  Shut it!

*Points at* CORRIE, *which stops* SNIFFER *abruptly in his drift. They stare for a few seconds.* CORRIE *continues to cry, wiping her face with her sleeve.*

Mam.

*Startled,* CORRIE *looks up at him with red eyes.* CUBBY *takes a cautious step or two towards her.*

Come on, mam. Give us knife.

*Step or two.*

Come on. Don't be daft.

*Step or two. He is now hovering over her.*

Gizzit to me now. Come on.

*He takes the knife out of her hand. She offers no resistance.*

Mam, it int that bad. What d'yer think you're up to?

*Pause.*

CORRIE:  What d'yer mean? I were only choppin' onions.

*Silence. Then* SNIFFER *bursts out laughing.*

SNIFFER:  Shouldn't do that, yer know. Do yersen a nasty.

CUBBY:  All right.

SNIFFER:  The unfortunate victim were in such a state, she choked 'ersen to death on onion fumes.

CUBBY:  Don't rub it in.

CORRIE:  This is a joke or summat?

CUBBY:  'S all right, mam. Take no notice. He's bein' daft.

*Inadvertently waves the knife about as* SNIFFER *comes past him on the way to the television.*

SNIFFER:   'Ere! Watch me onions!

CUBBY:   How d'yer gerron at 'ousin' benefits?

CORRIE:   Hmmm.

CUBBY:   Oh, no.

> SNIFFER *switches on television. Cowboys and Indians. He plonks himself down in front of it.*

CORRIE:   I went in there. I said: I can't pay me electric bill. They said: that's nowt to do wi' us. I said: aye, but you int payin' me rent, are yer? They said: so what? I said: while 'ousin' department tell DHSS I've paid up me arrears, DHSS wunt deal with electric board. D'yer know what they said?

CUBBY:   No.

CORRIE:   What's yer name? Aye, they did. They asked me flamin' name an' address.

CUBBY:   What d'yer say?

CORRIE:   Walked out, dint I?

CUBBY:   Yer what?

CORRIE:   Oh, I know I should've stayed, love. But it right got me, yer know. Fox, Fox, over an' over, an' still gerrin' nowhere.

SNIFFER:   Well, what abaht lecky?

CUBBY:   Hang on.

SNIFFER:   If it's cut off, we're buggered for wrestlin' Saturday.

CUBBY:   Leave it out. Can't yer see she's upset?

SNIFFER:   I'll be bloody upset if I miss me wrestling.

CORRIE:   I'm sorry, love. Doin' me best.

CUBBY:   Don', mam. All 'e thinks abaht's 'imsen. If 'e dint watch so much, we wunt 'ave such a big bill, anyway.

SNIFFER:  You like wrestlin' an' all.

CUBBY:  I don't march straight in t' 'ouse an' put telly on whatever.

CORRIE:  Quiet, the both o' yer. Gi' me 'eadache again.

CUBBY:  Tryin' to gerrim to switch it off.

CORRIE:  It dunt matter.

SNIFFER:  *(to* CUBBY*)*  See?

CUBBY:  What?

SNIFFER:  It dunt matter.

CORRIE:  Shut up!

SNIFFER:  Yeah. Shurrup. I'm watchin' telly.

CUBBY:  No, you're not.

*Switches set off.*

SNIFFER:  Yeah, I am.

*Gets up.* CUBBY *brandishes the kitchen knife.*

CUBBY:  Stab your eye.

SNIFFER:  Mam, 'e's threatenin' me.

CORRIE:  Cubby, put knife down for 'eaven's sake!

CUBBY *backs away from television.*

SNIFFER:  *(smirking)*  Nah! See?

*Swaggers to the set. Switches it on. A small but startling explosion. The stage is engulfed in blackness.*

What's 'appened?

CORRIE:  They've cut us off.

CUBBY:  No they ant.

SNIFFER:   I were right enjoyin' that film.

CORRIE:   What else can it be?

CUBBY:   They can't cut you off this time o' night.

CORRIE:   All they do is pull a lever or summat.

CUBBY:   Mam, they got to ask permission. They've got to come in an' fiddle wi' fusebox.

SNIFFER:   Permission? Well, that's friggin' stupid. Who's gonna say: Oh aye, come in, that's right, cut me lecky off, fine . . . Oh, an' d'yer wanna turn gas off while you're at it . . . an' we aint paid water rates so . . .

CUBBY:   They send police round, wazzock.

CORRIE:   What we gonna do?

SNIFFER:   Oh, shut it.

CUBBY:   'S all right, mam. Just sit down.

CORRIE:   I am sittin' down.

CUBBY:   It's probably fusewire. I'll take a look.

*Crash of furniture.*

Bugger!

CORRIE:   What, leave us 'ere? In dark?

CUBBY:   Won't be long.

CORRIE:   They've cut us. I know it.

CUBBY:   Mam, will yer stop fussin'? It don't help.

CORRIE:   They've done it. I knew they would.

CUBBY:   Look after 'er, Sniffy. Won't be a minute.

SNIFFER:   Don't call me that.

CORRIE:   I'll 'ave to go out.

CUBBY:   Eh?

CORRIE:   Get some 'elp.

CUBBY:   Mam . . .

CORRIE:   It's all my fault. I can't just sit 'ere doin' nowt. Alone in the dark.

SNIFFER:   There's me.

CORRIE:   'S what I mean.

CUBBY:   Sit down.

CORRIE:   I'll get some 'elp. Won't be long.

CUBBY:   Where from?

CORRIE:   Outside.

CUBBY:   Where, though?

CORRIE:   I dunno! I dunno! Out. Just out.

## SCENE NINETEEN

*Lights gradually build.*

SINGER:
Pity the Mohican mother
Bringing up Mohican brothers
Fatherless Mohican brothers
Pity the Mohican mother.

*The corner shop. She masks up as the* WOMAN WITH THE CROOKED NOSE. CORRIE *goes to her.*

CROOKED NOSE:   Hello, love. What can I do for yer?

CORRIE:   *(shaking)*   Do you do that paracetamol or owt?

CROOKED NOSE:   What for?

CORRIE:   Hedex. Owt. It dunt matter.

CROOKED NOSE:   Sorry, love. Don't encourage anyone to take drugs.

CORRIE:   Eh?

CROOKED NOSE:   Yer look pale, love. What's trouble?

CORRIE:   Oh, nowt much.

CROOKED NOSE:   Then yer don't need drugs, do yer? Won't catch me sellin' no-one rubbish they don't need. Go 'ome.

CORRIE:   It's me 'ead.

CROOKED NOSE:   Well, that's alright. Mug of Ovaltine. Two slugs o' Scotch. Head on piller. Right as rain in t'mornin'.

CORRIE:   Dunno if I got no Scotch.

CROOKED NOSE:   Off licence. Two blocks down. Now, come on. I'm closin'.

CORRIE *dithers.*

Be off wi' yer. I wanna close shop.

*Pause. Then* CORRIE *bursts into tears.*

Oh dear. Is it summat I said?

*Comes round the counter to console* CORRIE.

Tell us, love.

CORRIE:   *(crying)*   I must be a terrible mother.

CROOKED NOSE:   Now don't give me that, love. Ant 'eard so much rubbish for ages.

CORRIE:   But me two sons. They're gerrin' into trouble. They wear ridiculous clothes. An' their 'air – I dunno. It's all my fault, though. I just can't seem to . . . well, I don't know where the next money's comin' from.

CROOKED NOSE:   *(realisation)*   Oh, you're worried abaht your electric bill.

CORRIE:   They've cut us off. I 'ad to go. Couldn't stand it. Sittin' in dark an' cold . . . How d'you know?

CROOKED NOSE:   Well, you're not alone, are yer, love? Not on this estate. All electric bills come same day, dunt they? Who can pay on time round 'ere? The 'ole neighbourhood's threatened wi' disconnection regular, every three month. Surprised they even bother with individual customers. They ought to just go round the estate wi' tannoy on reminder day.

CORRIE:   Huh.

*Pause.*

CROOKED NOSE:   Listen, I could 'elp if yer liked.

CORRIE:   Help?

CROOKED NOSE:   Oh, aye. They all come to me for 'elp round 'ere. It's what a corner shop's for, int it? I'm not just a batty ol' woman, yer know.

*Pause.*

CORRIE:   What sort o' help?

CROOKED NOSE:   Well, better for yer than paracetamol, any road.

# SCENE TWENTY

*Lights fade to black. A torch beam picks out* CUBBY's *face from beneath.*

CUBBY:   I am the ghost o' mains electric!

SNIFFER:   Ah!

CUBBY:   I am the ghost of amps an' voltage!

SNIFFER:   Chuff off.

CUBBY:   Give yer a shock, eh? Shock. Gerrit?

SNIFFER:   Ha bloody ha.

CUBBY:   'Ere y'are. Cop this.

*Lights a second torch.*

SNIFFER:   What?

CUBBY:   Cop 'old.

*Gives torch to* SNIFFER.

Int fuses. Maybe it's telly.

SNIFFER:   Eh?

CUBBY:   Well, that's 'ow yer did it, wunt it? Buggerin' abaht wi' set. Come on. I'm takin' back off.

*Shining torch, he prods at the television with the kitchen knife.*

## SCENE TWENTY-ONE

CROOKED NOSE *leads* CORRIE *to a seat.*

CROOKED NOSE:   Ovaltine nice, were it?

CORRIE:   Aye. So were Scotch.

CROOKED NOSE:   Good. Now, give us your 'ands.

*Takes* CORRIE's *hands in her own.*

Now don't be frightened. I'm just gonna get yer right relaxed. Alright?

CORRIE:   *(slightly hesitant)*   Yeah.

CROOKED NOSE:   I just want yer to let your mind go.

CORRIE:   Go where?

CROOKED NOSE:   Nowhere. Just sort o' concentrate.

CORRIE:   What on?

CROOKED NOSE:  Nowt. Empty your mind,

*She closes her eyes, breathes deeply.* CORRIE *looks round, bewildered for several seconds.*

CORRIE:  I'm empty.

CROOKED NOSE:  Ssssh!

*Several seconds.*

CORRIE:  *(whisper)*  Is summat s'posed to 'appen?

CROOKED NOSE:  *(trance-like)*  O spirits of the Midewiwin . . .

*At this,* CORRIE *gives a little cry of shock which breaks* CROOKED NOSE *out of her trance.*

It's alright. It's alright.

CORRIE:  What yer doin'?

CROOKED NOSE:  Don't be scared.

CORRIE:  What is it? Looks like . . . one o' them . . . what d'yer call 'em . . . seance.

CROOKED NOSE:  It's alright.

CORRIE:  You're gonna do a seance? Just wi' me? Alone?

CROOKED NOSE:  Oh, you're never alone in a seance, love. That's the 'ole point of 'em. I'm allus callin' 'em up, me ancestors. Ask 'em to drop in for a little chat, like. It's nice to keep in touch with all your friends an' relations. Cheaper than British Telecom, any road. Yer see, I got this little Red Indian guide. Little boy Wakankan. 'E's allus comin' to see me wi' news from t'other side.

CORRIE:  Well . . .

CROOKED NOSE:  Look, love, I dunt play abaht with this. It's serious. There must be someone yer wish were still 'ere, that yer could lean on.

*Pause.*

CORRIE:  Aye. There is.

CROOKED NOSE:  Well then. Shut your eyes. An' dream.

*Takes her hands. Eyes closed,* CROOKED NOSE *breathes herself into a trance again.*

CROOKED NOSE:
O spirits of the Midewiwin
Spirits of the Menomini
Wonder workers of Winnbago
Medicine men of the Wapanachki
Do you have a message for us?
Are we now within your hearing?
Wa-kan ka-an yan wa-on we
Man-pi-ya ta wa-ki-ta ye
Is there anyone there?
Is there anyone there?

*Suddenly* CUBBY *and* SNIFFER *are bathed in green light.* SNIFFER *looks around, dumbfounded.*

SNIFFER:  Wha . . . What's 'appened?

CUBBY:  I dunno. I just . . . an' . . . It's magic.

SNIFFER:  Where are we?

CUBBY:  What?

SNIFFER:  Woodhouse Ridge, int it? All them trees.

CUBBY:  It's amazin'. Like Star Trek. 'Beam me up, Scotty.' Phhumm! In a forest.

SNIFFER:  Cubby.

CUBBY:  Mmmn?

SNIFFER:  Life int like Star Trek. Star Trek's on telly. *(Pause.)*  Yeah, it's Woodhouse Ridge. Must be.

CUBBY:   'T int.

SNIFFER:   'T is.

CUBBY:   There's too many trees. 'Sides. See that thicket? If yer look careful, yer'll see a great Canadian moose.

*Green light off. Television on. Cowboys and Indians.*

SNIFFER:   'Ere, Cubs. It's on. Telly. It's on.

CUBBY:   *(nonchalant)*   Yeah.

SNIFFER:   What d'yer mean, yeah? What's 'appenin'?

CUBBY:   Eh?

SNIFFER:   Forest. We were in a forest.

CUBBY:   What?

SNIFFER:   Woodhouse Ridge.

CUBBY:   You been sniffin'?

SNIFFER:   Yeah. No. What's goin' on?

CUBBY:   I been fixin' telly.

SNIFFER:   What were that abaht 'air gel?

CUBBY:   What?

SNIFFER:   Settin' gel. Yer just said it. Yer said: if yer look careful, yer'll see a great Canadian mousse.

CUBBY:   One of us 'as been sniffin', and it int me.

SNIFFER:   Yer did. A second back.

CUBBY:   Just 'elp us put this back on.

CUBBY *starts to replace the back of the television.*

CORRIE:   Are yer sure they're alright?

CROOKED NOSE:   What? Oh yes, I should think so. Looked
     'appy enough to me in that there forest. Good lookin' lads.
     If they dint make 'emselves up like a pair o' cockatoos.
     They'll turn out fine. Specially that eldest. Got spirit,
     anyway. 'E were in shop earlier. Tried pinchin' a few
     things. I wunt 'avin' that.

CORRIE:   Pinchin'? No!

CROOKED NOSE:   It's alright, love. They dint get owt. I pulled a
     gun on 'em. Everythin' went back on counter before yer
     could say, West Yorkshire Constabulary.

CORRIE:   Gun?

CROOKED NOSE:   Oh, nothin' dangerous. Just an old rifle o' me
     'usband's.

*She rounds the counter and takes out the rifle.*

He used to do a bit o' shootin' with it in t'old days. Yer
know, rabbits an' things. Well, 'e were a poacher, really.
Back before war, when everyone were out o' work.

*Thrusts rifle at* CORRIE, *who takes it at arm's length.*

I allus keep it 'andy, next to me wine gums.

CORRIE:   Yer were gonna shoot me kids?

CROOKED NOSE *snatches the rifle back.*

CROOKED NOSE:   Oh no, love. It int loaded.

CORRIE:   Pity. They deserve it.

CROOKED NOSE:   I mean, I just keep it for show, dunt I? A
     warnin' like. Just a warnin'. In case o' trouble. Oh yes. I
     mean, most kids are alright underneath bravado. Like your
     own. Just show 'em a barrel. They'll take the 'int.

CORRIE:   How am I gonna stop 'em pinchin'? They'll get put
     away.

CROOKED NOSE: *(waving rifle)* We-ell! Keep one o' these in your bottom drawer. Bit o' violence never did no-one 'arm.

CORRIE: They're criminals.

CROOKED NOSE: I know what folk say: it never 'appened in our day, all this fallin' off back o' lorries. Well, course it dint. They're wunt no lorries, an' them that there were, had nowt worth pinchin'. An' if yer did get summat, you 'ad nowhere to purrit. There were none o' these hatchbacks on cars. All yer could do were stuff it up your jumper – or down where your lad stuck a can of 'airspray.

CORRIE: Where?

CROOKED NOSE *nods suggestively.*

Oooh, no!

CROOKED NOSE: Honest, love. It were like a length o' drainpipe.

*They laugh.*

CROOKED NOSE: No. Your lads'll be alright. Now go 'ome to 'em, an' stop worrin'.

CORRIE: I can't go back to that dark.

CROOKED NOSE: I'll bet you owt, your electric's back on.

CORRIE: Eh?

CROOKED NOSE: You'll see. Go on. Get 'ome.

*Unlocks the door for* CORRIE.

An' come back to see me any time. 'Specially abaht that bill, eh?

CORRIE: Oh. Right.

*Goes to the door.*

Listen, thanks very . . .

CROOKED NOSE:  Sssh! No, no. Go 'ome, Corrie. An' get those lads sorted out, eh?

CORRIE:  Yeah.

CROOKED NOSE:  Mark me words, love. They'll grow up fine. Just like we did.

CORRIE:  Yeah.

*Hesitates, turns, goes.*

CROOKED NOSE:  God 'elp 'em.

## SCENE TWENTY-TWO

CUBBY *finishes replacing the back of the television.*

CUBBY:  Well, that's a job done. Amazin' what yer can do with a kitchen knife an' a bit of initiative. Yer know, if I ever 'ad to fend for mesen in wild, first thing I'd want for survival'd be a good knife.

SNIFFER:  First thing I'd want'd be me UB40.

CUBBY:  Yeah, well. You wunt sixer in cub pack, like I were.

*Gives knife to* SNIFFER.

SNIFFER:  Oh, Akela will be chuffed wi' yer.

CUBBY:  Aye. Good deed for day.

SNIFFER:  *(pointing at television)*  Look, 'ow did yer do that?

CORRIE *goes to them.*

CUBBY:  Hello.

SNIFFER:  Where you been?

CORRIE:  So it *is* back on.

CUBBY:  Lecky? Aye. Dunno what it were. Fuses were okay. So I decides to fiddle wi' telly. All of a sudden – phhumm!

Picture back on. Lights back on. Everythin'. Must've been a short or summat.

CORRIE:  She were right, then.

CUBBY:  What? Where yer been?

CORRIE:  *(deep in thought)*  Eh?

CUBBY:  Who yer been seein'?

*Silence.* CUBBY *and* SNIFFER *look at each other.*

SNIFFER:  Yeah, well. Now you're back, yer can get choppin' them onions. I'm starvin', me.

*Waves knife at* CORRIE.

CUBBY:  Careful!

CORRIE *does not bat an eyelid.*

SNIFFER:  You hear?

CORRIE:  It were another world.

SNIFFER:  Come again?

CORRIE:  I dunno. We were talkin' wi' a Red Indian.

SNIFFER:  Red Indian? What the 'ell she on abaht?

CORRIE:  Wakankan, the guide. An' the spirits o' Midi-wotnot. Listen, everythin's gonna be alright. She told me. She looked into future. You were walkin' in a wood. Yer were 'appy.

SNIFFER:  Wood?

CORRIE:  You're gonna be fine, she said.

SNIFFER:  What wood?

CORRIE:  She said electric'd be on. An' look.

CUBBY:  Mam, who's *she?*

SNIFFER:  I said, what wood?

CUBBY:  Not 'elpin', are yer?

SNIFFER:  She's pullin' uz leg.

CORRIE:  Power. She's got this sort o' power. The lights. Telly. It's a sign. Must be.

SNIFFER:  It's a set up. She's got a screw loose.

CUBBY:  What yer talkin' abaht?

CORRIE:  A friend.

CUBBY:  What friend?

CORRIE:  Someone yer both know.

SNIFFER:  Oh, no. No way. Me mates are mad, but they int insane.

CORRIE:  She spoke to these spirits. Should've seen it. Spirits from land o' dead.

CUBBY:  Mam . . .

*Approaches her slowly.*

CORRIE:  Nice spirits. Well meanin'. Oooh, it were marvellous. Wonderful.

CUBBY:  Mam, what's been goin' on?

*Touches her gently on the shoulder.*

SNIFFER:  It's a full moon. Must be 'er PMT.

CORRIE *slaps* CUBBY *hard across the face.*

CUBBY:  *(holding cheek)*  'E said it!

CORRIE:  *(suddenly on the offensive)*  You've been thievin' again, ant yer, you two?

CUBBY:  What?

CORRIE:   Come on. Don't try an' wriggle out.

CUBBY:   What d'yer 'it me for?

CORRIE:   Today. This afternoon. I've told yer not to, ant I?

CUBBY:   I said, why d'yer 'it me?

CORRIE:   Straight answer. Come on.   *(Turning on* SNIFFER*)*
An' you. If yer don't explain, you'll get one too.

SNIFFER:   Look, why dunt yer go rest? I'll do tea for a change,
like.

*Snatches up knife suddenly Holds it out in front of him
demonstratively.*

CORRIE:   Corner shop. Eh? Tell us, then. Ant I right?

SNIFFER:   Dunno what you're on abaht.

CORRIE:   No? S'pose yer dint 'ave a gun pulled on yer, neither.

SNIFFER:   Eh, who's she been yabbin' to?

CORRIE:   So yer know then.

CUBBY:   What she tell yer?

CORRIE:   Who?

CUBBY:   You know who yer mean, dunt yer?

CORRIE:   Do I?

SNIFFER:   Does she?

CUBBY:   Ol' bat in corner shop. What she been yakkin' abaht?

CORRIE:   Well, you should know, shouldn't yer?

*Pause.*

SNIFFER:   Look, mam. I dint wanna do it. 'E put me up to it.

CUBBY:   I tell yer, mam. Keep away from 'er. She's twisted.

CORRIE:    She made fools o' you two, dint she?

CUBBY:    What d'yer mean, fools? She's mad. Wavin' a gun
abaht. She could kill someone.

CORRIE:    It wunt loaded.

*Pause.*

CUBBY:    What?

CORRIE:    It dint 'ave no bullets in. It were just for show.

*Pause.*

SNIFFER:    She's lyin'.

CORRIE:    No, I don't lie. Remember? I ant got imagination.

SNIFFER:    Who said that? It wunt me that said . . .

CORRIE:    I never brought you two up to do owt like that. I 'ope
she's learnt yer a lesson. I 'ope you feel ashamed o' yersens.

*Pause.*

CUBBY:    *(quiet, brooding)*   I'm shamed up alright. Right
shamed up. Shamed I let mesen be taken in by owt like 'er.
An' you too. Me own mother conned by a freak like that
'cos we can't settle uz own differences. It's a disgrace to
family. Disgrace to the name Fox. An' I int 'avin' it. Come
on, Sniff.

*He storms off.*

SNIFFER:    What?

CUBBY:    Just come on!

*Exit.* SNIFFER *glances at* CORRIE *and follows.*

CORRIE:    *(shouting after them)*   Where yer goin'? What yer
gonna do?

# Scene Twenty-three

SINGER:

> Stay your hand, Mohican brothers
> Do not seek your confrontation
> Do not seek your instant vengeance
> It can only end in violence!

*Enter* CUBBY *and* SNIFFER. *They hammer on the door of the corner shop.*

CUBBY:   Come on! Let us in, you ol' cow!

SNIFFER:   What we gonna do?

CUBBY:   Just shurrup an' leave it to me, right?

*The* SINGER *masks up as the* WOMAN WITH THE CROOKED NOSE. *She comes to them.*

CROOKED NOSE:   Lads! What yer come to thieve off me this time o' night?

*They force their way past her into the shop.*

I'm shut.

CUBBY:   Yeah.

CROOKED NOSE:   Your mam popped in tonight.

*She manoeuvres herself between them and the counter.*

CUBBY:   That's why we're 'ere. What d'yer say to 'er? She's off 'er rocker.

CROOKED NOSE:   She is a bit upset, yes.

CUBBY:   Not surprisin'. What d'yer do to 'er?

CROOKED NOSE:   'Elped 'er with some problems.

SNIFFER:   You're 'er problem, missus.

CUBBY:   She's alright. We'll sort 'er out. She dunt need some busybody like you, pokin' your bent konk in.

CROOKED NOSE:   She say this?

CUBBY:   Never mind what she says. I'm tellin' yer. Right?

CROOKED NOSE:   If she wants to come, I'm not stoppin' 'er.

*She has positioned herself behind the counter.*

SNIFFER:   Want this shop sortin'?

*Goes for her,* CUBBY *holds him back. She produces the rifle from behind the counter, points it at them.*

CROOKED NOSE:   Now get out!

CUBBY *launches himself across the counter, grabs the gun, throws it to* SNIFFER.

CUBBY:   Yer can't try that on. It dunt work twice.

CROOKED NOSE:   Give it 'ere!

SNIFFER *is holding the gun up to his squinting eye, trying it out for size.*

SNIFFER:   Magic!

CUBBY:   *(to* CROOKED NOSE*)*   You're all bluff, int yer?

CROOKED NOSE:   Give us gun. It int a toy.

CUBBY:   Listen to me. Lay off our mam.

CROOKED NOSE:   Alright. Alright. Just give us gun.

SNIFFER:   What for? 'T int loaded, is it?   *(Makes noise like gunshot)*   Bggghh! Bggghh!

CROOKED NOSE:   What?

CUBBY:   Promise you'll stop interferin'. Then you'll 'ave it back.

SNIFFER:   Bggghh!

CROOKED NOSE:   I promise. Yes. Now, purrit down!

SNIFFER:   Bggghh!

CROOKED NOSE:  For God's sake, you'll do some 'arm!

SNIFFER:  Put a cork in it!

*Swings round suddenly, pointing the rifle at the* WOMAN.
*Freeze. Drum beat. Snap lighting change to red.*

CORRIE:  *(with tom-tom)*
He felt the trigger tighten
*(Beat)*  He saw the muzzle flicker
*(Beat)*  He heard the crack of cartridge
*(Beat)*  He smelt the burn of powder
*(Beat)*  He felt the shock of kick-back
*(Beat)*  The butt of fate on shoulder
*(Beat)*  And as an old life vanished

*Gunshot. The* SINGER *slowly removes her* CROOKED NOSE
*mask, and walks away from the scene.*

*(Beat)*  He sensed the taste of slaughter.

*Snap light change back to previous setting.*

CUBBY:  *(under his breath)*  Christ!

SNIFFER:  *(gibbering)*  She said it wunt loaded. Dint she? You
'eard. What she say that for?

CUBBY:  Gorra get out.

SNIFFER:  How was I s'posed to . . .?

CUBBY:  Come on. We gorra go.

*Grabs the rifle and makes to go.* SNIFFER *takes a step
towards the counter.*

SNIFFER:  She went . . . where'd she go . . .?

CUBBY:  For Chris' sake, run!

*Grabs* SNIFFER *and drags him away.*

SNIFFER:  Where'd she go?

# SCENE TWENTY-FOUR

*Alarm bells.* CUBBY *and* SNIFFER *dash hither and thither
about the stage, hunted animals on the hoof. Voices. Shouts.
Finally, the fugitives arrive beside the level which served as
the shop counter. In mime,* CUBBY *wrenches open a car door
and jumps onto the level as if it were the driver's seat. He
reaches over, opens the passenger door, furiously beckons*
SNIFFER *to get into the vehicle.* SNIFFER *hesitates as a siren
swells into life, distant.* CUBBY *becomes visibly angry.*
SNIFFER *gets into the car.* CUBBY *turns the ignition, starts the
engine at third or fourth attempt. They lurch off,* CUBBY
*using steerer and gears like a rally driver. Siren noises
approach. The cold blue pulse of a police car light. Car chase
sounds. Radio messages bleed across the airwaves.* CUBBY
*gives nervous glances to his mirrors.* SNIFFER *bites his nails,
tugs at his locks, looks to side and behind. From these
naturalistic mannerisms, they develop a relatively formal
but anxious little dance. They start to gesture and point,
clearly arguing about directions.* SNIFFER *tries to grab the
wheel.* CUBBY *throws him aside, but as he does so, loses
control of the steerer. They throw their arms across their
faces. Screech of brakes. Deafening impact of machinery
against masonry.* CUBBY *and* SNIFFER *hurl themselves
forward onto the floor. Flash of lights, followed by
blackout.*

# SCENE TWENTY-FIVE

*Light builds slowly. Shafts of green. Silence, punctuated
only by the whispering rush of a distant stream, and the
occasional hoot of a night owl. A forest at night.* CUBBY *is
sitting up.* SNIFFER *comes round, clutches his head.*

SNIFFER:   Where are we? Ow!

CUBBY:   Hurt?

SNIFFER:   Like a drum beatin'.

CUBBY: You 'it dashboard. 'Ad to drag yer out. But I covered tracks.

SNIFFER: Where is this?

CUBBY: Safe. For a while.

SNIFFER: Ridge? Woodhouse Ridge, is it? That's where we were 'eadin' when . . . Christ, did I really . . .?

CUBBY: Ssssh! Gotta keep quiet.

SNIFFER: Kill 'er? What'll they do to me? What'll they do?

CUBBY: Quiet. Chris' sake. They int gonna catch yer. Right?

SNIFFER: It's murder . . . I dint mean to . . .

CUBBY: They don't know who you are. Yer wunt get caught. 'Sides, a Fox is too cunnin', right? They'll never find us. An' if they do, we'll fight 'em to last. *(Grips rifle.)* No. They'll not shoot a Fox in the forest.

SNIFFER: Shoot?

CUBBY: We'll wait while midnight . . . all clear . . . then back to lair.

SNIFFER: What d'yer mean, shoot? *(Pause.)* Cubs? *(Pause.)* I'm starvin'.

CUBBY: I'll find some food.

*Rises.* SNIFFER *starts to do so.*

SNIFFER: I'll come wi' yer.

CUBBY: No. Stay 'ere. Risky enough, one of us goin'.

SNIFFER: *(pointing to the gun in* CUBBY's *hands)* Takin' that too?

CUBBY: Course.

SNIFFER: What for?

CUBBY:    Food.

   *(Pause.)*

SNIFFER:    What'm I gonna do?

CUBBY:    Get some sticks. We'll make a fire.

SNIFFER:    They'll see us.

CUBBY:    No-one'll see us 'ere.

   *Turns to go.*

SNIFFER:    Cubby.

CUBBY:    What?

SNIFFER:    Is it really Woodhouse Ridge? Don't look right.

CUBBY:    No. An' if yer listen careful, yer can 'ear a coyote cry,
   an' a heron in t'marshes.

   *Exit.*

SNIFFER:    What?    *(Goes after him)*    'Ere, Cubby! Oooh!
   *(Winces, puts hand to his bruised head.)*    Maybe it's a
   nightmare. Bonk on head.    *(Wipes his hands down his
   face, shivers, pulls his jacket round himself, rubs his palms
   together.)*    Brrr.    *(Sings a pop song.)*
   'New York, ice cream
   TV, travel
   Good times
   Norman Wisdom . . .'

   *(Looks up, around)*    Hello!    *(Pause.)*    Who's there?
   *(Shivers.)*    Sticks for fire.    *(Looks about, sees pile of leaves
   and branches, starts collecting sticks, notices something
   strange, picks from the pile a wooden arrow with brightly
   coloured feather-flights. Looks at it in amazement for
   several seconds. Suddenly looks round)*    What's that?
   *(Pause.)*    Who's there?    *(Pause.)*    Cubby? That you?
   *(Looks again at the arrow, throws it down, paces, sings.)*

'New York, ice cream
TV, travel
Good times
Norman Wisdom . . .'
*(Looks up. Pause.)*   Sod it!   *(Sits down, produces from his
jacket a can of Evostick and a polythene food bag. Removes
lid from the glue can. Opens the neck of the bag wide. Starts
to pour the slime into the plastic. Gunshots, distant.* SNIFFER
*looks round startled, puts glue and bag down carefully,
leaps up.)*   Cubby? Cubs?   *(Looks round helplessly)*   Oh
Christ.   *(Runs across in the direction of the shots.)*
Cubby? What if 'e's . . .?   *(Looks round again. Hesitates.
Returns to his solvent session. Thrusts his head into the
turned-back opening of polythene, and breathes heavily.
The bag expands and contracts like an artificial lung.
Suddenly, he looks up again, waits, continues with his fix,
inhaling much more furiously. Forest sound atmosphere
builds slowly to claustrophobia.)*

*Enter* CUBBY. *He stands there resplendent in traditional
Mohican costume: scalp-lock decorated with shells and
beads (wampum), and feathers. Naked torso daubed with
greasepaint. Deerskin breeches and moccasins. Tomahawk
slung from belt. Jewellery. From one hand hangs a freshly
shot rabbit, from the other the rifle.* SNIFFER *looks up.*

SNIFFER:   King Ada!

*Looks at his glue bag as if to say, 'that must be good stuff'.*
CUBBY *rushes across and snatches the bag away.*

SNIFFER:   Wha . . .?

CUBBY *points in the direction from which he came. He sniffs
the air and at the ground. He thrusts the polythene pouch
and glue can into* SNIFFER'S *arms.*

SNIFFER:   Uh?

CUBBY:   *(pointing)*   Yengeese.

CUBBY:   Yengeese. Paleface.

> SNIFFER *shakes his head.*

Blue coats.

SNIFFER:   *(feigning comprehension)*   Oh!

> CUBBY *pulls* SNIFFER *to his feet.*

SNIFFER:   What abaht nosh?

CUBBY:   Come.

SNIFFER:   Listen, Cubs, can we go 'ome now?

> CUBBY *drags* SNIFFER *away.*

# SCENE TWENTY-SIX

> *Tom-toms.* CUBBY *and* SNIFFER *journey through the forest.*

SINGER:
>It is not the swiftest beast a-
>Foot that stays the longest distance
>So wild foxes flee the chase by
>Stealth and wiles and sheer resistance
>Through the spruce wood, through the pine glade
>Sniffer sees his sometime brother
>Finding north by moss on beech-bark
>Or, in clearings, starlit skymap
>Little Sniffer, cold and hungry
>Lost in nightmare night of forest
>Wonders . . .

SNIFFER:   Is this cunnin' bugger really our kid Cubby? Bloody
. . .

> CUBBY stops in his tracks. SNIFFER *bumps into him.*

Oh!

> CUBBY *puts forefinger to lip. He points at* SNIFFER's *boots.*
> *Motions him to remove them.*

SNIFFER:  *(whisper)*  Eh?

> CUBBY *demonstrates removing boots.*

> Take me boots off?

> CUBBY *nods.* SNIFFER *gives glue bag and pot to* CUBBY, *sits down, removes his boots.*

> It's soakin'.

CUBBY:  Trail.

SNIFFER:  Nowt to trail these socks'll leave. 'Ad 'em on all week.

> CUBBY *tucks the glue bag and pot into the boots, gives them back to* SNIFFER. *They journey on. Tom-toms.*

SINGER:
> Keeping space between their trackers
> And themselves, the pair trek onward
> Foxes hounded by their hunters
> Foxes holding dogs at bay by
> Leaving earth beneath them traceless
> Showing a clean pair of heels
> Soon they reach a limestone cliff-face
> Dropping down towards a river . . .

> CUBBY *and* SNIFFER *stop.* CUBBY *points.*

SNIFFER:  *(horrified)*  Down there? I can't get down there. I got weak knees.

> CUBBY *beckons.*

SNIFFER:  Do we 'ave to?

> *A loud noise off.* SNIFFER *starts.* CUBBY *listens.*

SNIFFER:  What's 'at?

> CUBBY *pulls up his scalp-locks and makes chopping movements across his forehead.*

Scalp? What, mine yer mean?

*They scramble across rocks. Tom-toms.*

SINGER:
　　Down the rocks the Foxes clamber
　　Down the cliff-face to an inlet
　　In which, hidden by a steep bank
　　Drifts a black canoe of birch-bark

CUBBY:　In!

SINGER:　Mohican says to brother

CUBBY:　In!

SINGER:
　　. . . as if their lives depended
　　On this boat, or they'd be straddled . . .

SNIFFER:　Up the creek without a paddle.

　　CUBBY *squats on the level, pulls* SNIFFER *in behind him to simulate the canoe.* CUBBY *rows with his rifle as if it was a paddle. Tom-toms. Sounds of cataracts and waterfalls.*

SINGER:
　　Silently, the birch-bark gliding
　　Under skilled Mohican guidance
　　Under limestone cliffs and caverns
　　Through ravines where treetops totter
　　'Til it reaches whirling eddies
　　Where the river turns to rapid
　　But the helmsmanship at bow-end
　　Never puts the boat in danger . .

　　*Waterfall sounds.* CUBBY *holds the canoe steady, stands, jumps ashore, turns quickly, pulls the canoe to the bank.* SNIFFER *jumps ashore.* CUBBY *catches him, points to a cavemouth.*

SNIFFER:   What's this? Ugh! Not goin' in there. It's all dark an' 'orrible.

CUBBY *drags him on.*

SNIFFER:   Listen, what . . .?

*Noise off.*

CUBBY:   In!

*Drags* SNIFFER *down behind a rock. A second or two.* CUBBY's *head appears with rifle at the ready. Then* SNIFFER's *head appears.*

SNIFFER:   Look, this int Woodhouse Ridge, is it? I mean, we int nowhere near Leeds really, are we?   *(Pause.)*   What's going on? You're not really me brother still, are yer?

CUBBY:   All Mohican brothers. All tribesmen brothers, 'til last of us go to land of spirit. White man master of Earth. But time for red man will come again.

*Pause.*

SNIFFER:   Oh. That's okay, then.

SNIFFER *yawns.* CUBBY *smiles at him.*

SNIFFER:   'S all t'excitement.

CUBBY *shuts his eyes in posture of sleep.*

CUBBY:   Blackstone soft.

SNIFFER.   Yeah.

*Emerges from behind rock and lies down. Sleeps. To him, the* SINGER, *as the* WOMAN WITH THE CROOKED NOSE.

CROOKED NOSE:   Sniffer! Sniffer Fox!

SNIFFER:   *(waking)*  Uh!

CROOKED NOSE:   It is I. The woman with the crooked nose.

SNIFFER:    But you're dead, int yer?

CROOKED NOSE:    As dead as yourself. And as alive.

SNIFFER:    I can't cope with this.

CROOKED NOSE:    It were a good hit, lad. Straight to the heart.

SNIFFER:    Yer shouldn't 'ave said it wunt loaded.

CROOKED NOSE:    Fear not, I seek no revenge. I know you are in torment and I come to pacify. It is Mohican fate to live in sorrow and pain. But now I am delivered to the vale of spirits. And soon, you yourself will join us in these happy hunting grounds.

*Goes.*

SNIFFER:    'Ere wait! Tell uz summat!

*Noises close.* CUBBY *suddenly springs into action, gun at the ready.* CUBBY *beckons* SNIFFER *to join him behind the rock.* SNIFFER *scrambles across.*

SNIFFER:    Thought yer said we were safe.

*Silence. Then, from some distance, a bluff Yorkshire accent growls through a megaphone.*

VOICE:    Alright, lads. Now let's be sensible. My boys 'ere 'ave got yer surrounded an' covered.

SNIFFER:    Pigs!

VOICE:    Now if yer can just do this quiet an' calm, everythin'll be alright. So let's start wi' yer throwin' your weapon out where we can see it.    *(Pause.)*    Now, come on, lads. Let's not 'ave any trouble.

SNIFFER:    What's 'appenin'? What'll we do?

CUBBY:    Mohican brave fight to death.

SNIFFER:    There'll be 'undreds of 'em. SAS.

CUBBY:   Mohican brave proud.

SNIFFER:   What?

CUBBY:   Mohican brave no afraid.

SNIFFER:   This Mohican brave afraid. Let's run for it. Christ, they'll murder us!

*CUBBY does not flinch.*

VOICE:   Alright, lads. 'Ave it your own way. I'll give yer one minute to come out with your 'ands over your 'eads.

*Long silence.*

SNIFFER:   What the 'ell yer waitin' for?   *(Pause.)*   Christ, will yer tell me what's goin' on? Who are they? Is it pigs? Tell me, can't yer?   *(Pause.)*   For Chris' sake, who are yer? Not me brother, are yer? Are yer? Christ, where am I?

*Grabs CUBBY. CUBBY pushes him away.*

VOICE:   Thirty seconds.

*Silence.*

SNIFFER:   Right, I'm givin' messen up.   *(Pause.)*   Look, we can't just sit 'ere. They think I'm a killer!

*He makes a grab for the gun, wrestles with CUBBY for it, wrenches it from CUBBY's grip, rushes out into the opening waving it.*
It's alright! I gorrit . . .
*Deafening volley of gunfire. Light change. Freeze. SNIFFER caught in a moment of terror.*

# SCENE TWENTY-SEVEN

*Tom-toms. Wailing. Lamentations. CUBBY comes up behind SNIFFER, who sinks back into his arms. CUBBY lowers him reverentially to the floor, removes the gun, arranges the body. CORRIE comes downstage, raises her right hand.*

CORRIE:    I swear by Almighty God that the evidence I shall give
shall be the truth, the whole truth, and nothin' but the
truth . . . Mrs Cora Alice Fox . . . 13 Hudson Terrace . . .
Woodhouse . . . Leeds 6 . . . separated . . . unemployed
. . . mother of two sons . . . sorry . . . one son . . .

*She breaks down.* CUBBY *stands, goes to her, leads her across
to the body. She stands above it, strews it with forest
flowers.*

SINGER:
So departed little Sniffer
Little Sniffglue, scarce beloved
But, for that, a true Mohican
Sole of foot to spike of scalp-lock
All who have not hearts of blackrock
Weep now for these broken people
'Til these tear-swept isles of Britain
Bury deep their last Mohican!

*Tom-toms. Wailing. Lamentations. Slow fade to black.*

# *Toby and Donna* (Louise Page)

## Interview with the author

*Where did the idea come from?*

> I was asked by the BBC to write a short play that raised issues of debate for young people.

*Why did you choose the issue raised by* Toby and Donna?

> It seemed an issue that is difficult to discuss – especially at home. It is something easier to discuss among your peers.

*How old were you when you wrote it?*

> Twenty-eight.

*Did you draw on your own experiences?*

> Yes, partly. But there are also things you understand, say, by standing at bus stops at night and hearing conversations going on between kids. You somehow know it is the sort of thing going on all the time. I think a writer tends to absorb the things that happen around her or him.
>
> I'm thinking of those conversations – and it's not just teenagers and kids – where people are forcing other people into things. You know – it's all dressed up, but the manipulation goes on. And you can understand it is manipulation and you think you'll be able to get out of the situation . . . But it's sometimes hard to get out.

*Do you think Donna is going to get out of it?*

> The play is open-ended. If she 'gets out of it' she's open to a lot of other dangers. Walking for a cab, or whatever. She's in a difficult position, a woman out on the streets at

that time of night. I don't think he's going to suddenly say, 'I'll walk you home'. If *she* were seducing *him*, of course, he'd have a lot more options open.

It's easier for boys.

*Are you a feminist?*

Yes, it's the way I live my life. I myself am the sort of feminist who wears a dress – what Fay Weldon calls a 'frockie'.

*And is it a feminist play?*

No, it's a people play. For people.

*Do you think you're fair to the boy?*

I am in this particular play. I wouldn't say all men are like this but I don't think he behaves very differently from a lot of other men. I've certainly been in situations like the one Donna is in, with the men assuming that, eventually, you'll say 'Yes'. So it seems perfectly legitimate to write about a man behaving in the way Toby does.

*What do you hope the play might do for young people working on it?*

What I'd like them to do is to realise how innocently things can begin. Not just the sexual adventures – but the manipulation that goes on generally. The way we all tend to trade with various bits of our life. Donna realises what's going on. The bells start ringing. Things aren't quite as they seem. She thinks she can get out of it – it's quite fun. And she realises the pressures – 'Let me seduce you or I'm not going to see you again'.

That's a huge fear for any young girl – that sense that you are nobody without a boyfriend, and if you're not out on a Saturday night you're a social outcast. (I now realise it's wonderful staying in on Saturday nights!)

I didn't talk at sixteen about that sort of thing. The

conversations had a huge subtext, of course, but they were very superficial. You might talk about your parents but you'd never really discuss how you felt as a boy or a girl. And it was particularly hard to discuss things without accepting all the peer-group pressure. I used to loathe discos at that age – it took me a long time to realise I could just not go.

*Young people of that age might be talking about your play now?*

Well, it was written as a play to be used, to be talked about and to open things up. I'd be very happy if they said, 'Let's write our own version' – about what might happen the next time Donna and Toby meet, or perhaps finding a way in which Donna could get Toby to discuss her point of view.

*There might be some difficulties for young people in actually performing this play. Could they?*

Yes.

*You don't think they might find Toby and Donna too much like themselves?*

That shouldn't be a problem. They're different people. You have to become those different people.

You approach it the same way a writer does – looking at it as a different situation from the ones you've been in, but similar. You have to step into different people's shoes, and create something different. When you write, you think people will recognise things about you in what they read. But they don't. So it's like saying, 'My name is Jane but in the play my name is Donna. So I now need to find out about her, what she does and what her world is'.

And you know, when the lights come up – you can't see the audience.

## Advertising the play

You work in the publicity department of the theatre that intends to perform this play. You are told by the director that the title isn't catchy enough. It won't result in 'bums on seats' (audiences).

● Discuss a new title with some of your colleagues. You have to agree on one in exactly quarter of an hour, because the printer must have the copy then.

● You have room for exactly seventy-five words, to advertise the play, with its new title, in the publicity hand-out. Write them. You might begin: 'At last – a play for young people that really tells us how it is to be young. Take one girl and one boy . . .'

## Reading the play

How easy was it for your group to read the play? Were some people embarrassed? How did it show? What did it show?

Louise Page was more than ten years older than her teenage characters. Had she forgotten what it's like to be in this situation?

● Discuss in groups, appoint a spokesperson, and report back.

## Casting the play

● In small groups, cast the parts of Toby and Donna from:
(a)   soap operas on the telly;
(b)   famous young people;
(c)   characters from other books and plays;
(d)   your school/college/youth club; and
(e)   amongst yourselves.
Compare casting decisions.

# *Exploring the text*

After the read-through, the director should start to 'move' the play. The actors now have to get up and start acting, and decisions have to be made about how to do it.

The most obvious way of performing this (and any) play would be to present it like real life ('naturalistically') – with real sofas, televisions, etc. This might not be the most rewarding way of presenting some plays.

● In pairs, as co-directors, work out a way of performing the play 'non-naturalistically'. (For instance, you might arrange it so that the actors never actually touch, or you only have one item of furniture; or . . .)

● Test out your ideas on parts of the play.

Louise Page says she'd be happy if you wrote your own version of the story.

Actors and playwrights often work towards a better understanding of what is in the play by improvising or writing different versions and extra scenes, to find out what their characters are like, in different circumstances and with different people.

● Find out what happens when:

  (a) Susan meets Donna at the disco, the following Saturday night;
  (b) Toby's mother comes home to Toby on Sunday morning;
  (c) Toby meets Donna again;
  (d) Toby's mum gives Donna another lift;
  (e) Toby meets Donna's dad.

● Sometimes it helps to try scenes the other way round – suppose (as Louise Page suggests in her interview) that it is the girl who has set out to seduce the reluctant boy, late on a Saturday night . . .

• Read parts of the play with a male Donna and a female Toby.
  Plays keep changing their meaning, even when they are
actually in performance. Even the same actors on successive
nights, using the same lines and the same movements, can find
that the play changes. And, of course, different actors and
different directors can change what happens very considerably.

• Work in groups of three. One person in each group takes the
role of the director and gives secret notes to each actor about
how they are to play the scene – to be especially kind, say, or
stupid or gentle or ignorant or selfish or shy or drunk . . .
As actors, read sections of the play, each obeying your secret
instructions. Discuss the results.
  The play's structure seems quite simple – Donna and Toby
talk, cuddle and quarrel at the end of an evening together; he
wants her to stay the night, she doesn't want to.
  But who tells the story (i.e. who is the narrator)? And what
difference does that make? (Suppose Donna doesn't understand
some things? Suppose she is not always speaking the truth?)

• Discuss in groups, and report back.

• Read the play again, this time without any of Donna's 'asides',
where she speaks directly to the audience. How does that change
the play?
  Louise Page's play doesn't include Toby's thoughts about the
events of this Saturday night. But it might help actors, working
on the script, to find out more about what Toby is up to, to try
the following exercise.

• Two actors read the play again, missing out all Donna's asides
to the audience. A third actor inserts Toby's thoughts as the
scene proceeds.
  For example, the opening might be:

TOBY:   We were standing at the bus stop and she was staring,
    not talking or anything, and I said

    You've missed it.

DONNA:  I haven't. It doesn't come while five to.

TONY:  Gone that.

DONNA:  It hasn't.

TOBY:  I looked at my watch, which is rather clever because it lights up in the dark so you can read it at five to twelve at night, and I know she thinks it's daft but she can't tell the time in the dark like I can.

*(To* DONNA*)* Four minutes to. I tell you, it's gone early.

And it's not my fault we missed it, either. They do Saturday nights, so they don't have to pick up drunks coming out at closing time.

DONNA:  Give it a bit longer.

TOBY:  I kicked about a bit and she stared down the road as if that'd make it come. I didn't want it to have gone. What was I reckoned to do? Not much of a Saturday night, this.

*Pause.*

I'm bored.

● Write up a key page of the play, with Toby's thoughts added.

## Looking at the characters

### Toby

Does Louise Page like Toby? Do you? How do we make him a real, dramatic character instead of what he might easily become – a rather stereotypical male?

● Make a list of all the speeches where you think he is lying.

We hear Donna's thoughts in the play; we don't hear Toby's. But the actor playing him must know what they are, even if he never says them (and even if the playwright doesn't say them, or perhaps doesn't know them, either).

In rehearsals, the actor playing Toby and the director would have to decide fairly early on exactly what Toby was really up to on this Saturday night (Donna wouldn't necessarily need to be in on this discussion).

• In pairs, in role, with one of you as the director and one the actor playing Toby, discuss the character; what is known about him, and what must be 'discovered' to make him real. Has he, for instance, intended to seduce Donna?

Go through the play together, reading only Toby's lines and making notes of the key things he says.

• Discuss whether Toby loves Donna. He says he does. But exactly when does he say so? And why?

Does he really 'fancy' her? And if he does, why hasn't he (apparently) tried anything all night, when they have been alone together in the house?

What has his 'relationship' with Donna been, up to this Saturday night?

• Swap roles of director and actor and probe a little deeper into what's going on in the play. You may have decided earlier that Toby tells lies. But is he telling the truth, for instance, when he says he's had very little sexual experience? ('Have you been with other girls?' 'Well . . . ' 'Well?' 'No'.) Donna can't know if this is the truth. But Toby would know – and the actor playing him will need to 'know' as well, if he is to make sense of his character.

And there are other questions for the director and actor to discuss. For example, Toby seems to have a broadminded mother, but hasn't she taught him anything important about the 'facts of life'? He's wrong when he says girls can't get pregnant the first time they have sex. Hasn't his liberated mum told him? If she has, why is he pretending to Donna? Doesn't he really care about Donna at all? Why hasn't he got any condoms? Why hasn't she? Why has it suddenly got to be about 'going all the way'?

The director might choose to widen out from the play itself in the search for Toby's 'character'. One way might be the 'hot-seat' exercise. For this, the director asks all sorts of fairly random questions, many not answered in the play, and probably needing intelligent guesswork, as the actor builds up the sort of person he thinks Toby must be. ('Do you play football?', 'What's your favourite band?', 'Do you get on with your mum?', etc.)

- Play the hot-seat game on Toby.

- Using all your notes on Toby, write a character portrait of him.

- Compare all your pictures of Toby.

## Donna

In the play, Donna talks directly to the audience as the evening develops. In fact, she must, of course, be talking about it with the benefit of hindsight. But what do you think happened afterwards?

- Re-read Donna's final speech, 'He just looked at me', etc. Louise Page says the play is open-ended. But is it? (The actor playing Donna will need to know, won't she?) Read the speech, first on the assumption that Donna is going to say 'Yes', and then again, assuming that she is going to say 'No'.

- Write the synopsis of what *you* think happens next. For example:

'Donna says she'll have another drink. Toby says he's sorry, he does love her, he was being horrible. But all the lads at school talk about it, and anyway, she will talk about it and tell everyone and make him look a fool for not trying. She . . . ' (etc.).

- Re-read the last part of the play, with Donna knowing what you have now made up for her in the future. What difference does it make?

• Work in pairs. A friendly teacher has found Donna very upset at school on Monday. Donna tells the teacher what happened on Saturday. The teacher tries to fill in what she hasn't been told. (Do you love Toby? Did you? Did you like him? Fancy him? When exactly did you realise what he intended? Why didn't you want to stay? Really? What sort of 'relationship' had you had up to that Saturday night? You must have kissed him – you knew he was a 'lovely kisser'. Why were you *frightened* (one of the few stage directions of the whole play on page 26)? Should you have been? He seemed to blame you – he said, 'after the way you've just treated me' – were you to blame at all? You misled him a bit, didn't you? What next? What have you learned from it all? Etc.)

Write up the diary of Donna, aged 15¾. (We meet; we go out; that Saturday; the next time we met; saying sorry; too late; etc.)

## After the curtain comes down

Louise Page says *Toby and Donna* is a 'people play', and though she is a feminist herself, this is not a feminist play . . .

('Feminism – a doctrine or movement that advocates equal rights for women'. – *Collins English Dictionary.)*

• Discuss in pairs and report back. What do you understand by 'feminism'? Are there members of staff you assume to be 'feminists'? Ask them what they believe? Where did they get their ideas from? What people influenced them in deciding what they believe about equality for women? When did they decide? Can they help untangle what Louise Page says about being a 'frockie'? Do you have to be a woman to be a feminist? What would a person who said, 'I am not a feminist', believe? What do you believe about equal rights for women?

• Role play, in threes.
    Three people have seen the same performance of the play. One regards herself as a 'feminist', one as a 'sensible ordinary

person' and one as a 'male chauvinist'. The three meet to discuss, on TV or radio, what they have seen.

● Working in threes, tape record the discussion. And then, compare tapes from the other groups. These notes might help you find the three different 'roles', e.g.

– you are a strong feminist. You think the play *is* feminist but doesn't go far enough. (Look at the order of the names in the title, for instance? And why aren't the women more supportive of each other? And the play doesn't tell us half of what goes on when boys start manipulating girls, etc. Donna has to grow up and see what the world's really like.)

– you are a 'sensible, ordinary person' who thinks it is daft talking about things like feminism when it's just a story about what happened between two kids. (You don't go to plays to be told what to think. People see things in plays that aren't there. Donna needs to grow up and see what the world's really like, that's all.)

– you are a male chauvinist (pig). (You are irritated by the way the play portrays men (dads, men in the hotel, as well as Toby himself) as villains, and excuses women, who know exactly what they're up to, really. Donna (and Louise Page) should grow up.

● Toby's seduction technique is a bit primitive when you look at it closely, isn't it? Baths and new shirts and so on? In one column, list his tricks; in the other, list Donna's responses to these tricks, e.g.

| HIM | HER |
|---|---|
| if you loved me you would . . . | if you loved me you wouldn't try to force me by saying you love me |

Donna feels trapped (and Louise Page says it's a common feeling when you're young) in that, if she doesn't do what she doesn't want to do, she won't have a boyfriend and she won't be able to go out on Saturday nights. What advice do you have about that? What should be done about it? How could things be made easier between boys and girls of this age?

● Work out together 'twenty ways you didn't know of saying, no' for a tabloid newspaper. (E.g.  1   Always make sure you can get home safely, by having a bike and carrying a portable telephone.)

● Toby and Donna spend part of the next day writing letters to an advice columnist in a magazine. Write the letters, and the replies.

● Discuss together other songs, poems, sayings, films, or stories, that deal with similar matters to those in Louise Page's play, and compile an anthology that would help anyone working on *Toby and Donna*.

Louise Page says the play was written deliberately to deal with 'issues for debate' for young people, and she suggests that the issues are not only about how girls might be manipulated in matters of sex, but that people get manipulated in other ways too. How well do you think the play deals with the issues?

● Tell the story of how you, or someone you know, was manipulated.

# *Lily and Colin* (Elisabeth Bond)

## Interview with the author

*Where did you get the idea for* Lily and Colin?

We had a room in the house in Lancaster where I lived. It was used as a night shelter for the homeless – a small 'doss house', you might say – that was used by all kinds of people, but mainly ex-prisoners. They were inadequate people, who should never have been locked up. We had a call from the police one afternoon. A policewoman came round with a little girl – I think she was called Lily, actually.

She'd had a much older boyfriend and they had been living rough at the nearby motorway services station. He'd been picked up by the police for impersonating a policeman – directing the motorway traffic into the service station. They'd been sleeping in a phone box. She said, 'He were only trying to help'.

She'd gone beserk, gone like an animal; demented at the thought of being separated from him. And she was brought to us. The policewoman was really concerned. She said she'd have to send her back to Leeds to her dad. The girl said, 'He'll only beat me up'. And she stayed the night. She was absolutely filthy

That was the story thrust under the playwright's nose . . .

*What did the playwright do with the story?*

*Lily and Colin* is the second play of a trilogy. The first one was called *Lily on the Grave*, based on a hostel.

In the first play, Lily and Colin meet and decide to go

away. And I fell in love with the two characters. I got excited by the possibilities of writing about an alternative that worked – an alternative to the norm, like a relationship between a thirteen-year-old girl and a thirty-eight-year-old man. It was a relationship that worked blissfully well. But you can't have people behaving as they behave – and I wanted to ask, why not?

I also wanted to write about what we expect, i.e. the lifestyle we demand (some people can't manage without a microwave). Lily and Colin's expectations are so low. In the light of them being thrilled by the prospect of eating Stork rather than catering margarine, I wanted to query our own expectations.

*What happens in the whole trilogy?*

*Lily on the Grave* was a stage play about them meeting. The third one has Colin in prison in London and Lily goes down to London, having absconded from her children's home, and survives on the streets. Colin comes out of jail and they try to make it together, and it ends very tragically. Colin turns on her, and she ends up in prostitution.

There was a five-year gap between the writing of the first play and *Lily and Colin*. The version here is for the radio. I also adapted it as a film, and the BBC did it as a telly play.

*Have you finished now with the two characters you say you fell in love with?*

Yes – Colin rounds on Lily and it's the end. I'm quite sad.

*What happens when playwrights fall in love with their characters?*

You always need to keep your objectivity. I've once or twice got too emotionally involved.

*Lily says she likes the way Colin speaks – but they both speak in a rather unusual way?*

> Lily's fairly normal – a streetwise Lancashire toughie. I write naturalism, but I'm interested in how far you can push it.

*What about Colin? Where did you find him?*

> He's not based on anyone I know. He's religious because it's a handle to hang him on. His speech pattern became difficult on the last play, I couldn't take it any further.

*Some people might regard the play as being immoral?*

> It always amazes me how easily people are offended. They don't want to know what the world is really like. The play doesn't suggest Lily and Colin's is the right way to behave. It says, 'There are alternatives to a man marrying a woman three years younger than him, getting a semi, having two kids'.
>
> It says, our so-called norms are a bit strange.

*There might be some Lilys who'll read this play. What about the effect on them?*

> It's not an artist's problem, is it? The responsibility is to the art. It has to be, doesn't it?
>
> It's a very moral play. It's a story that shows that human beings, whatever their disadvantages, have a capacity for love. It's about pure love. Love, not sex. You can still hang on to love, however awful the circumstances. But they don't gain anything by it.

*Your vicar doesn't have much love, does he?*

> He's a decent liberal – would you want Lily and Colin to come and stay in your home?

*And the police?*

> They over-react in the play, don't they? But somebody has to stop people burning things down and scratching fourteenth-century church doors. I wanted to raise the questions . . . plays don't answer questions, they raise them.

*Are there other influences on the play?*

> I suppose – Sean O'Casey. But no, not on *Lily and Colin*, I don't think.

*Are you yourself in some ways the 'Lily' of your plays?*

> Not in the actions but yes, there's a bit of me in Lily.

*Like?*

> I hope I have her ability to be starry-eyed. I hope I never lose it. And I like the idea of running away – it would be nice to pick up your bag and run away, wouldn't it?

## Advertising the play

● The publicity department at the theatre don't think the present title will get 'bums on seats'. Instead of *Lily and Colin*, you need to come up with a new title. In exactly quarter of an hour the posters are going to be printed . . .

1  Set an alarm clock for fifteen minutes from now.

2  Individually search through the play, for five minutes, jotting down quotations that could make titles (e.g. 'Don't You Want Us To Be Happy?').

3  Spend the remaining ten minutes discussing and voting – and finally choosing a new title, before the alarm rings and it is too late.

## Reading the play

Elisabeth Bond says she is amazed by how easily people get
shocked. Were you shocked? Did the play seem immoral to you?
Do you think it could cause harm to people reading/acting/
watching it?

● You are editing a book of plays for use in schools and colleges
and you begin to worry about objections to some of the contents
of *Lily and Colin*. Censor the five most 'offensive' things in the
play. Compare cuts.

● Discuss in groups, and appoint a spokesperson to report back,
one or all of the following:

1  'There might be some Lilys who'll read this play. What about
the effect on them?' 'It's not an artist's problem, is it?'
2  'It's a very moral play. It's a story that shows that human
beings, whatever their disadvantages, have a capacity for love.'
3  'Plays don't answer questions, they raise them'.

Commenting on whether this play is really suitable for students
like yourself, a teacher said: 'Because youngsters of this age are
exploring their own identity they often react unfavourably to
characters which don't conform to their norm. Some may simply
recoil because Colin is 'weird' and Lily is nevertheless attracted
to him'. Do you recoil? Is the teacher right?

## Exploring the text

The script of *Lily and Colin* in this book is the radio version.
You are adapting it for performance in front of a live audience.
Go through the play, noting all the settings.

● Design the basic setting for a live performance of the play –
deciding how many rostra, microphones, screens, etc., you
might need; and what furniture and props in each. You might
find you wish to make this as simple as possible (see, for

example, the 'setting' Garry Lyons chose for his play, *Mohicans*, as described on page 180).

● Display these different settings and discuss how well they might work.

● Using a map, chart the journey of Lily and Colin. Does it matter where the play is set? To you? To the characters? To the playwright? How would it be different if the places were all made up?

● The *News of the World* gets hold of the story of Lily and Colin. Collect and display tabloid newspaper headlines/stories about tragedy in the lives of ordinary people. Discuss the display.
   Examine in detail how the tabloid journalist and his (or her) sub-editor report such a story. (You might be able to find cuttings from more than one paper dealing with the same story – including, possibly, an account from one of the 'quality' papers.) How many words are allowed for dealing with such tales? What does the opening paragraph do? How long is each paragraph? What are the 'emotive' (colourful) words, used to entice the reader? What do the headlines, picture and 'crossheads' do – to the story and to the reader? What might the 'true' story be?

● Write the headline for the *News of the World* version of Lily and Colin (e.g. 'GYMSLIP RUNAWAY AND THE NIGHT THE VICAR SAID NO').

● In the same number of words as a real newspaper account, and using the same kind of language, write up the story for next Sunday's issue. Which account is more 'truthful' – that of the play or the newspaper? How do you think this exercise might help in the preparation of a production of the play?

● Some people might be surprised by the amount of humour in a play that deals with such dark matters as *Lily and Colin* (e.g. Lily's account of the insurance man and the fires, page 79). List five moments, speeches, events that made you laugh. Compare lists.

● Discuss why you think Elisabeth Bond chose to include this humour in her play? Does it weaken the play?

● There is a lot about religion in this play. Look back over the play, noting all the references to religion. In one page, sum up what Colin believes about God.

● Improvise – Colin and the prison chaplain meet across a table to discuss God. (The chaplain might begin by saying, 'Well, Colin, we have a few minutes to be quiet together and to talk about some important things. Tell me what you believe about God?').
Replay the scene in the play with the vicar. What are your feelings about him?

● 'Maybe God's in there, calling out to us: "Come in Colin and Lily, come in out of the rain." ' In groups, discuss why God doesn't give more help to Colin and Lily in this play. Report back to the other groups.
    The play is just too long for a new collection of plays about to be published. You have to cut twenty or so lines. Your editor suggests cutting the reference to 'Trident' and 'Maggie' (p.69) and the stuff about the secret nuclear train and 'Maggie' (p.76). (p.68).

● Give your answer to these suggested cuts. Offer alternative cuts, if necessary.

## Looking at the characters

### Lily and Colin

'I've never met anyone like you, Lily', he says. And she replies, 'I've never met anyone like you'. Have you met anyone like either of them?

● You are actors, trying to build up your characters. You think of other people you have known who might at least have some similarities to Colin or Lily. Cast yourself as one of them.

● Brainstorm for five minutes, jotting at great speed on a piece of paper all the people you have known, in real life and in fiction, in books and films and on the television, whose lives and behaviour and ways of speaking might give you some clues to your character. Compare the results of the brainstorming.

● The playwright calls Lily and Colin 'inadequates'. Do you agree? Are there better descriptions? Compile a list for Lily and for Colin of ten phrases, sentences or speeches that best sum up the kind of people they are (e.g. Lily: 'I'm unshockable'; 'Me, I'm bursting wi' goodness'; etc.). Compare lists.

● 'I've not even started in my dreams yet', says Colin. Make up a dream for Lily or Colin. (It might help to draw/paint it. Or a poem might emerge . . . )
    A case conference is called the week after Colin and Lily have been separated by the police. The question is, 'What shall we do with Lily?'. Among those invited to turn up at the case conference on Lily, are:

  – one of the social workers from the play;
  – one of the policemen from the play;
  – the policewoman;
  – the vicar;
  – Lily's father;
  – one of Lily's teachers;
  – Lily's aunt;
  – others.

● Work in groups. Each choose a role, prepare one piece of evidence you need, and then have the case conference, with whoever turns up . . . and decide what to do with Lily.

● During the car ride away from Lily, Colin Beaumont is very surprised to find it is all a mistake and he is really being kidnapped in order to appear on the television programme, 'This Is Your Life'. Various people from his life suddenly reappear to tell their stories of him, and to meet him again (e.g. Rev. Arthur Philpott, the lorry driver with the smelly socks, etc.). Re-enact

Colin Beaumont's surprising appearance on 'This Is Your Life'.

● Tucker (p.37), Lily's father (p.48) and the vicar (p.70) have monologues. Make up a similar monologue for either Colin or Lily at the very end of the play.

Elisabeth Bond's last play about Lily and Colin ended with them parting, for ever. Is that the ending you would have chosen if you were the playwright? Would you have been disappointed if you had been in the audience?

● Write the scenario for a fourth play about Lily and Colin (set, perhaps, some years ahead, when they meet again . . . ).

### The other characters

There are many other characters in *Lily and Colin* but we only really care about the two runaway lovers.

● Choose one of the 'authority' figures in the play and re-read what they say and do. How sympathetic is the playwright to them? Are they mocked or criticised in the way that they are portrayed (e.g. the vicar with the dog, or the social workers in the pub?). Does the playwright suggest in any way that the authority figures are the ones who are 'inadequate', really? Leading thin, dull lives, compared with Colin and Lily?

● Write up a report on either the vicar, the policemen, the social workers or the guard, recommending that they are taken away and locked up for being 'inadequate'.

## After the curtain has come down

● Lily and Colin, on the run together, have gone into the theatre to hide and keep warm. They have watched a play called *Lily and Colin*. What did they think of it?

# *M o h i c a n s* (Garry Lyons)

## Interview with the author

*Where did the idea for* Mohicans *come from?*

> I was working on a youth drama project with Major Road
> Theatre Company in West Yorkshire. I went to a run-
> down council estate in Batley, and met a group of
> unemployed teenagers with experiences of glue sniffing.
> Some of their personal stories are used in the play,
> transmogrified – like Cubby's description of the glue trip
> on page 104.
>
> I was looking for a play suitable for northern youth
> clubs, and I was very interested in trying to develop a
> particular theatre style exciting to people in their late teens.
> I wanted it to look different from a conventional play –
> picking up things in youth culture they were familiar with,
> but not treated in an obvious social – realistic way. I
> wanted to use that part of young people's imagination that
> rock music and fashion appeals to. Rock videos, for
> instance, were still quite new when I was writing it.

*How did it go?*

> It was a very long tour of one-night stands to youth clubs
> and some more conventional theatres. It has an immediate
> impact – it was written in a very upfront style.

*What do you mean 'upfront'?*

> It's a straight at the audience. That's so the actors can
> handle all the surprising things that can happen in a youth
> club.

*How?*

> You could freely improvise if the situation got out of hand
> – a bit like Shakespeare. But I was also concerned that it
> should be a play, rather than a working men's club act.
>    It stirred up a lot of debate critically. There were some
> comments about, 'What have contemporary punks got to
> do with Red Indians?, and, 'It's a bit of a gimmick'.

*When did you get the idea of linking up Red Indians with modern
punks?*

> When I got the title – very early. The haircuts in 1981–2
> were known as 'Mohicans'. There was a newspaper article
> – I'd been reading a lot about youth subcultures – in the
> *Guardian* about Mohican haircuts and youth in the North.
> Though actually, it's not a Mohican haircut – it's Mohawk.

*The Mohican name is connected with* The Last of the Mohicans
*– a novel by Fenimore Cooper about their extinction. Do people
need to know that?*

> Our audiences didn't. But some knowledge might be useful
> if you're studying it. Not the full story, but the feeling – a
> 'received feeling' we have about Red Indians, who we
> should call 'American Indians', by the way. And it's there
> in 'Hiawatha' too – a lilting, plaintive lament for a past
> civilisation – the noble savage. It's a very strong
> mythology. The play is about the similar passing of the
> inner-city working class, and our feelings of nostalgia
> about that.

*A 'lament' you call it?*

> Yes. But really it's a black comedy – the sad, plaintive
> mood's there, but the play's critical of it by cracking gags
> about it.

*The play was very successful with young audiences – but you got complaints about the language, and the glue sniffing?*

The language didn't come up as much of a problem. And for this published version of the play there have been only a very few word changes. There was a bit of trouble with the glue sniffing – not as much as we were expecting.

We reckoned by the time the play went out that it took a moral stance on it – saying, 'no'. And we also reckoned, I think rightly, that any kid who'll have tried glue sniffing will know how to do it, and lots of other kids will as well – and that anyway, it's most unlikely a kid will want to go and try it after seeing *Mohicans*.

There were only really problems in Kent, where the play was banned by the County Council Youth Service.

*What happened?*

They wanted to ban it and they found a way. They hadn't read it, or seen it.

They didn't like the title. And they'd probably heard rumours – the play had been done in London by then and had its reviews and all. They talked about the bad language, and it was pointed out there was very little. So then they said it was a political play and they didn't want that, and we said it was a social play and they said they didn't want that either . . . and then there was the glue sniffing.

*It is a political play.*

In the broadest sense. But it doesn't endorse a particular party line. You can draw your own conclusions.

*It went on to be a television play for Yorkshire TV – how difficult was that?*

They made quite a bold decision to film it all outside, and I adapted it for that. It was a good idea in televisual terms but . . . It lost a lot in terms of the richness of the magical, ritualistic quality. The stage version played up against these stretched Indian hides, grubby brown colour, and the stage floor was light browny woodland. It was like 'Hiawatha' – storytelling, oral epic. You were immediately in a magical context, nothing to do with the North of England.

Telly went the opposite way, for the social realism. And that left them a problem with the ending.

*In what way?*

They pulled out – I pulled out, under duress – the witch doctor bit in the middle – all that spiritual stuff. Which meant there was no motivation into the surreal switch to the New England woodland. So on telly it was purely on the basis of a glue-sniffing hallucination.

Now, in the stage play, it could be glue – but equally it could be a trip to the other world – imaginative storytelling with all sorts of dimensions and a much richer conclusion. If it's just a glue trip, it belittles the imaginative ending – and the whole reason for 'Hiawatha', and the American Indian resonances there.

*What advice do you have for people who might want to do a new production?*

Go with the style of the piece – don't try to find a recognisable reality – street-life reality. It appears to be about a couple of streetwise lads, but it's actually not that. It isn't a piece of documentary, though early on it gives the impression of being that.

When I was working on it, I used to walk into record shops for hours on end and look at the record covers. I let my mind go the way the designers of the record covers do – not getting hidebound with TV soap-opera reality, rooms, walls and so on, and the way real people are supposed to behave in most drama.

*What about the women?*

Ultimately – it's a man's play; in some ways, quite a male

play. Morally speaking, the women are the strength,
though – the shopkeeper women with the crooked nose is
the moral heart of the piece. She's the cornerstone of the
community.

And you have to remember the context of where it was
performed.

*You mean you were frightened of the lads in the youth clubs not
behaving when they watched it?*

Basically – yes. I felt I had to write a strong physical show.
It was the first youth-club show I'd written, and I'd not
then got a very great experience of youth clubs, either. I
wanted it to have a lot of energy, and it did appear to me
then that I'd get that through male characters rather than
female ones. I've subsequently discovered other ways.

But having hit upon the idea – a very captivating one
(the Mohicans idea) – I was naturally let into the male-
oriented American Indian mythology.

And there was the other chestnut of size of casts – I
could have had some female Mohicans in there if I'd had a
cast of eight, instead of four. That's just a question of
money.

*And 'Crooked Nose' – was that in there to keep the youth club
lads watching.*

No . . . the Iroquoian mask – a mask with a crooked nose
in Hiawatha's tribe, also wiped out – was put on in ritual
communications with the dead. It's a very vigorous image
in itself, though, of course, you don't need to know where
it came from when you're watching the play . . . That too
is very much part of the campfire storytelling style of
American Indian life, and of the play.

## Advertising the play

● Write a letter to the Organiser of Kent Youth Services. You have just read *Mohicans* and wish to offer your opinions about why it should (or should not) be banned.

## Exploring the text

Garry Lyons says that the idea for the play came from a newspaper article about the North of England fashion for American Indian haircuts – and the realisation that there were two sorts of Mohicans. His play merges the two.

1   On one level, there is a fairly simple story of what happened to two unemployed brothers in the North of England. Tell that story as simply as possible. (You might begin, 'Once upon a time, there were two brothers . . . '. And then you might finish '. . . and that was how it ended happily ever after').

2   There is the other level to the play, involving American-Indian history and mythology. To understand how the play works, we shall need to follow the trail the playwright leaves, deep into the lost cultures of the American Indian, real and as imagined by paleface writers – including Garry Lyons.

● Brainstorm yourself – that is, write without stopping or 'thinking' – for five minutes, writing absolutely everything that comes into your free – associating mind about 'Red Indians'. (If it helps, start with this list: Red Indians, smoke signals, squaws.) Collate everything on the American Indian, real and imagined, that your group collects by this brainstorming.
● Get hold of copies of Henry Wadsworth Longfellow's 'The Song of Hiawatha' (1855). Sit on the ground, American Indian campfire style, and tell the epic stories aloud.

By the shore of Gitche Gumee,
By the shining Big-Sea-Water,
Stood the wigwam of Nokomis,
Daughter of the Moon, Nokomis.
Dark behind it rose the forest,
Rose the black and gloomy pine-trees,
Rose the firs with cones upon them;
Bright before it beat the water,
Beat the clear and sunny water,
Beat the shining Big-Sea-Water . . .

• Spend a session in the library, finding out whatever there is to be found there of the customs and skills and strange death of the American Indian.

• A further part of the playwright's research for *Mohicans* involved mooching around record shops, looking at LP covers. Mooch around and look at LP covers. Report back on what you find in whatever way suits you best (e.g. a painting, a poem, a list, a photomontage, etc.).

Using an actual LP cover, discuss what 'images' (pictures and ideas) are used. Discuss what they seem to suggest, and what connections they have with the LP itself, and why they were chosen. Can you see how this sort of work might have helped Garry Lyons create his play?

• Agree on what should go into a display from (1) newspaper and magazine cuttings about what young people are getting up to in the cities – and their style and habits; and (2) the American Indian research.

Garry Lyons says that some people found the idea of comparing the 'passing of the inner-city working class' and the genocide of the American Indian 'a bit of a gimmick'. Do you understand what he means? Do you think it's 'gimmicky'?

Would you rather have just read a play that was 'TV soap-opera reality, rooms, walls and so on'?

• Search the stock cupboards for copies of the stage version of *Billy Liar* by Keith Waterhouse and Willis Hall. Compare Waterhouse's tale of northern youth from a generation ago, with that of Garry Lyons. What has changed in the northern youth scene? And what has changed in the way plays are written? Do you also find some similarities? (Whose sympathies are the authors with, for example?)

How do you think a play written about the urban young in the 1990s might be different? (Will there be full employment? Will the young be more obedient? Will they have a clearer sense of how they fit into things? And will stage plays themselves be different? Will 'live theatre' survive?)

Is there a sequel? *Mohicans 2*? What might happen? What would get missed out? How much of Cubby and Sniffer's talk would have to be cut?

• Discuss in groups one or all of the statements below. Appoint a reporter, who will tell the others in a plenary session what their thoughts were.

'There is nothing to lament for in the demise of the urban working class, if they were people who led lives like Cubby and Sniffer.'

'The American Indians lost, and they deserved to. Civilisation moves on.'

'*Mohicans* makes a lot of fuss about nothing very new – and has nothing really to do with American Indians at all.'

## Designing the set

Look at the 'setting' outlined at the start of the play. Why the leaves and the branches? And the stretched hides? Why do you think Garry Lyons reduced the world of his play to these particular articles?

● Make a list of the other visual effects there are, as the play proceeds.

● Design another setting that would be more suitable for a theatre or hall with which you are familiar.

## *Looking at the Characters*

● Working in threes, explore the characters of Cubby, Sniffer and Corrie. (Use the 'hot seat', improvisations, time charts, magazine photographs of faces that would fit, or anything else that will help, guessing where necessary, but including whatever the play actually tells us about them.)

● Write up the police report on one of them. For example, Corrie Fox, 46. Married, separated. 'Cubby' and 'Sniffer', her two sons, 19 and 17. Born in . . .

● Try some 'genre transformation' – this is where you adapt, say, a film into a poem, a novel into a play, etc. Devise 'The Ballad of Sniffer and Cubby', turning the play into a ballad song. (You might find it helps to use the tune and rhythms of a song you know.)

● Garry Lyons stresses, in the interview, how important he thinks the 'Woman with the Crooked Nose' is. She represents the older values – the women's values, perhaps – in a brutal men's world. Go through the play again, noting every reference to her – what she does and says when she is on stage. What values *does* she represent? How 'real' is she, compared with the Foxes? Do you think she does what the playwright says she does?

● Suddenly, it is possible to add four more women actresses to the company. What parts will you create for them?

● Draw up a new cast list, with the new actresses incorporated.

- Write the new synopsis of the story, including them.

- Write one of the new scenes.

  How is the play changed by adding more women? Does it make it better?

  What difference to the play does the part of the 'Singer' make? And who *is* this person, anyway? How much does the Singer know of what is coming next? Has the Singer got any 'characteristics'. (e.g. a sense of humour, anger, etc.)? Why 'singer' rather than 'narrator'?

- Read all the Singer's dialogue. In the Singer's style, make up some verses, celebrating something much more trivial – say, your young brother's birthday, or the night the telly went on the blink, or someone's first date.

## Rehearsing the play

At the final dress rehearsal, you discover that *Mohicans* is running ten minutes too long – and unless you cut it, the audience will all be leaving to catch the last bus as the play reaches its climax.

- You must cut 100 lines of the play, and you have only twenty-five minutes to do it in. Start the clock and make the cuts, with whatever discussion you have time for.

## After the curtain comes down

Garry Lyons mixed two apparently unconnected ideas in writing *Mohicans* – the present-day tale of two tearaway lads in Leeds and the much older epic of the death of the American Indian.

- Note five new ideas for plays, stories, poems or songs, using such unlikely mixing.